CALEB ROSS

Microservices Design Patterns For Serverless Application

A Complete Guide to sererless Application Design

Contents

Introduction: The Evolution of Serverless Microservices

The Shift from Monoliths to Microservices

For much of software development history, monolithic applications dominated the landscape. These systems were characterized by their large, unified codebases where various functions and services were tightly coupled. While monoliths were easy to deploy and manage in the early days, they soon became unwieldy as applications grew in complexity. Over time, the limitations of this architecture became apparent, especially as businesses demanded faster iteration, scalability, and flexibility.

Monolithic architectures, by design, bind all application components together, making scaling difficult and inflexible. Imagine a traditional online retail application built as a monolith. Every component—the product catalog, user authentication, payment system, and order management—is tightly integrated into one large codebase. This design worked well in the early stages of application development, but it quickly exposed its weaknesses as the user base grew and the platform became more complex. A single change in one part of the system, such as an update to the payment gateway, might require a complete redeployment of the entire application. Moreover, the inability to scale individual services based on demand led to performance bottlenecks and higher costs.

To resolve this, microservices architecture emerged as a revolutionary approach. In a microservices-based system, the application is broken down into small, independently deployable services. Each service is responsible for a specific business function and communicates with other services over well-defined APIs. For example, in our e-commerce system, the payment processing service can be separated from the catalog service and user authentication service. These independent services are typically deployed, maintained, and scaled on their own, leading to higher resilience, fault tolerance, and development velocity.

Microservices offer significant advantages over monoliths:

- **Independent scalability**: Each service can scale independently, meaning that the payment system can scale differently than the catalog service based on traffic demands.
- **Fault isolation**: A failure in one microservice does not necessarily bring down the entire system. If the payment service fails, the rest of the system continues to function.
- **Faster development cycles**: Teams can work on different microservices in parallel, allowing for quicker updates and releases.
- **Technology flexibility**: Microservices can be built using different programming languages and technologies, providing the flexibility to choose the best tools for the task at hand.

However, microservices also introduce complexities, particularly in terms of deployment, coordination, and communication between services. This is where the emergence of serverless architecture has helped simplify the process.

What is Serverless Architecture?

Serverless architecture is a cloud-native model that abstracts infrastructure management, allowing developers to focus on writing code without worrying about provisioning, scaling, or maintaining servers. The term "serverless" is a bit of a misnomer—there are still servers involved, but they are managed entirely by the cloud provider. In a serverless environment, developers simply upload their code, and the cloud provider automatically handles everything else, from infrastructure scaling to security updates.

At the heart of serverless computing is **Function as a Service (FaaS)**. In a FaaS model, developers write functions—self-contained units of code that execute a specific task—and deploy them to a serverless platform like AWS Lambda, Azure Functions, or Google Cloud Functions. These functions are event-driven, meaning they are only triggered by specific events (such as an HTTP request or a database update) and run for the duration of the task. Once the task is complete, the function terminates, and no resources are consumed until the next event occurs.

One of the most attractive features of serverless computing is its **pay-as-you-go** pricing model. Unlike traditional infrastructure, where you pay for computing resources 24/7 regardless of usage, serverless only charges for the actual time your code is running. This cost efficiency, combined with the automatic scalability of functions, makes serverless architecture a powerful option for modern applications.

Key characteristics of serverless architecture include:

- **No infrastructure management**: Developers no longer need to worry about provisioning servers, handling security patches, or configuring load balancers.
- **Auto-scaling**: Serverless platforms automatically scale functions based on demand, ensuring that applications can handle traffic spikes without manual intervention.
- **Event-driven execution**: Functions are triggered by events, reducing the need for always-on servers and minimizing resource consumption.
- **Built-in high availability**: Most serverless platforms are designed to be highly available, with automatic failover and redundancy built into the system.

Serverless has revolutionized the way developers think about deploying and managing applications, but it truly shines when combined with microservices.

Why Microservices and Serverless Are a Perfect Match

Microservices and serverless architectures share many fundamental principles, making them an ideal pairing for building modern, scalable, and cost-efficient applications. The modular nature of microservices aligns perfectly with the event-driven, function-based execution model of serverless platforms.

1. **Decoupling and Independence**:

- Microservices are inherently decoupled, meaning that each service operates independently of the others. Serverless further amplifies this decoupling by allowing each microservice to be deployed as a separate function or group of functions. For example, a user authentication microservice could be implemented as a series of AWS Lambda functions that handle login requests, user registration, and session management. These functions can be updated or scaled independently without affecting the rest of the application.

1. **Scalability**:

- Microservices require careful orchestration to scale effectively, but serverless abstracts much of the complexity. Serverless platforms automatically scale individual functions based on demand, ensuring that resources are used efficiently and applications remain responsive. In a traditional microservices setup, scaling would involve manually provisioning additional instances for each service, but with serverless, the platform takes care of this dynamically.

1. **Event-Driven Design**:

- Serverless functions are designed to be triggered by events, making them a natural fit for event-driven microservices architectures. For example, an order processing microservice can be triggered by an event such as a new order being placed in a shopping cart. Once the event occurs, the serverless function executes the necessary logic, processes the order, and stores the result in a database. This approach simplifies the design of microservices, allowing them to respond to specific triggers without the need for complex message queues or polling mechanisms.

1. **Pay-per-Use Efficiency**:

- Both microservices and serverless architectures emphasize resource efficiency. With serverless, you only pay for the actual execution time of your functions, which can lead to significant cost savings for applications with varying or unpredictable traffic patterns. This model aligns perfectly with the microservices approach, where individual services can be scaled and optimized separately. For instance, an analytics service that processes data overnight can remain idle during the day without incurring costs, while a high-traffic API service can scale dynamically during peak hours.

1. **Flexibility in Development**:

- In a serverless microservices architecture, developers have the flexibility to choose the best tools and technologies for each service. One microservice might be built using Node.js, while another is written in Python. Serverless platforms support a wide range of programming languages, allowing teams to leverage the strengths of different technologies without being tied to a single language or framework. This flexibility encourages innovation and allows developers to experiment with new technologies in a modular, risk-free environment.

By combining microservices with serverless, developers gain the benefits of both paradigms: the modularity and fault tolerance of microservices, and the cost efficiency and scalability of serverless. Together, they enable businesses to build highly responsive, scalable, and cost-effective applications that can adapt to changing demands.

Key Benefits of Combining Microservices with Serverless

The integration of microservices and serverless architecture delivers several key benefits that make this combination appealing for modern software development:

1. **Cost Efficiency**:

- The serverless pay-as-you-go model ensures that you only pay for what you use. This is particularly beneficial for microservices, as each service can scale independently, and you only incur costs when the services are in use. For example, if you have a microservice that handles user notifications, it only runs (and incurs costs) when notifications need to be sent. During periods of inactivity, no resources are consumed, leading to significant savings compared to traditional server-based microservices.

1. **Automatic Scaling**:

- One of the biggest challenges in microservices architectures is managing scalability. With serverless, this becomes a non-issue. Serverless platforms automatically scale functions in response to demand, ensuring that your application can handle traffic spikes without manual intervention. For example, if a flash sale causes a surge in traffic to your e-commerce platform, the serverless functions responsible for handling product searches and checkout will automatically scale to meet the demand.

1. **Simplified Deployment**:

- Deploying microservices traditionally involves managing servers, containers, and orchestrating deployments. Serverless simplifies this process by abstracting the underlying infrastructure. Developers can deploy individual microservices as serverless functions, and the platform handles the rest. This not only reduces operational complexity but also speeds up the deployment process, allowing teams to iterate faster and release new features more frequently.

1. **Fault Tolerance and Isolation**:

- In a microservices architecture, the failure of one service should not bring down the entire application. Serverless enhances this fault tolerance by providing built-in redundancy and automatic failover for functions. If a function fails, the serverless platform can automatically retry the operation or trigger alternative workflows. This isolation ensures that failures in one part of the system do not cascade to other services, improving the overall reliability of the application.

1. **Faster Time to Market**:

- With serverless, developers can focus on writing code rather than managing infrastructure. This accelerates the development process and allows teams to bring new features and products to market faster. In a microservices environment, this agility is further enhanced by the ability to develop and deploy services independently, enabling parallel development and reducing bottlenecks.

1. **Enhanced Developer Productivity**:

- Serverless platforms take care of infrastructure management, scaling, and security, allowing developers to focus on building features and improving the user experience. By removing the need for server provisioning and maintenance, developers can spend more time writing code and less time managing infrastructure. This increased productivity is especially valuable in microservices environments, where the complexity of managing multiple services can be overwhelming without automation.

1. **Global Availability**:

- Serverless platforms are designed for global distribution, with functions running in data centers around the world. This makes it easy to deploy microservices that serve users in different geographic regions, ensuring low-latency access and high availability. For example, an application that serves users in both North America and Europe can deploy serverless functions in data centers near each region, reducing response times and improving the user experience.

1. **Environmentally Friendly**:

- Since serverless functions only run when needed and scale dynamically, they consume fewer resources than traditional always-on servers. This leads to lower energy consumption and a reduced carbon footprint, making serverless microservices an environmentally friendly choice for businesses looking to reduce their impact on the planet.

By leveraging the strengths of microservices and serverless, businesses can build applications that are more efficient, scalable, and resilient than ever before.

Who Should Read This Book?

This book is designed for software developers, architects, and cloud engineers who are interested in building modern, scalable applications using microservices and serverless architectures. Whether you are new to serverless computing or have experience with microservices, this book provides the knowledge and tools you need to design, deploy, and manage serverless microservices effectively.

- **Developers**: If you are a developer looking to enhance your skills in microservices architecture and serverless computing, this book will guide you through the process of designing and implementing microservices in a serverless environment. You will learn how to leverage serverless platforms like AWS Lambda, Azure Functions, and Google Cloud Functions to build scalable, cost-efficient applications.
- **Cloud Architects**: For cloud architects, this book provides best practices and design patterns for building serverless microservices architectures.

You will gain insights into how to design scalable, fault-tolerant systems using serverless technologies, and how to integrate them into your existing cloud infrastructure.

- **DevOps Engineers**: DevOps engineers will benefit from the sections on automating deployment, monitoring, and scaling serverless microservices. The book covers tools and techniques for building CI/CD pipelines in a serverless environment, as well as strategies for ensuring high availability and fault tolerance.
- **Product Managers**: If you are responsible for managing the development of cloud-based applications, this book will help you understand the benefits and trade-offs of using microservices and serverless architecture. You will learn how these technologies can improve the scalability, reliability, and cost efficiency of your products, and how to guide your team in implementing them.
- **Tech Enthusiasts**: Even if you are not directly involved in building serverless applications, this book offers a deep dive into the latest trends and technologies in cloud computing. It will provide you with a comprehensive understanding of how serverless and microservices are shaping the future of software development.

By the end of this book, you will have a solid understanding of the core principles of microservices design patterns in a serverless context, and you will be equipped with the tools and knowledge to build efficient, scalable, and resilient applications.

Chapter 1: Introduction to Microservices in Serverless Architecture

Defining Microservices

Microservices architecture, often referred to as microservices, represents a significant shift in how software applications are designed and developed. At its core, microservices are an architectural style where a large application is broken down into smaller, independent services that can be developed, deployed, and scaled individually. Each microservice is responsible for performing a specific business function, and they communicate with one another over well-defined APIs.

In traditional monolithic architectures, all components of an application are tightly coupled, meaning they share the same codebase, deployment process, and runtime environment. This tight coupling can become problematic as the application grows, making it difficult to maintain, scale, and update. Microservices address these issues by introducing a modular approach where each service is autonomous.

To fully understand microservices, it's important to grasp their key characteristics:

1. **Autonomy**: Each microservice operates independently, allowing developers to modify, test, and deploy services without affecting the rest of

the system. For example, an e-commerce platform might have separate microservices for handling payments, user authentication, and product management. These services can be updated or scaled independently based on the demands of the business.

2. **Single Responsibility**: Microservices adhere to the **Single Responsibility Principle (SRP)**, which states that a service should have only one reason to change. Each service is built to fulfill a specific business requirement. For example, a payment processing microservice would only handle payment-related tasks, leaving user authentication or product catalog functions to other microservices.

3. **Decentralized Data Management**: In a microservices architecture, each service often manages its own database. This decentralization of data prevents the system from becoming a monolithic data store that's prone to bottlenecks. For instance, a shopping cart service would have its own database independent of the inventory service, allowing each to scale and operate independently.

4. **Communication via APIs**: Microservices communicate with each other through well-defined APIs, often using protocols like HTTP/HTTPS, gRPC, or message queues (like RabbitMQ or Kafka). These APIs are the "contract" between services, ensuring that services can interact without needing to know the internal details of each other's implementation.

5. **Polyglot Programming**: One of the major advantages of microservices is the ability to use different programming languages or frameworks for different services. Since each microservice is isolated, developers can choose the best tools and technologies for each service. For instance, you might write a real-time chat service in Node.js while using Python for a machine learning-based recommendation system.

6. **Independent Deployment**: With microservices, you can deploy services individually, without needing to deploy the entire application. This allows for faster iterations, quicker releases, and easier rollbacks if a service has a bug or performance issue. Each microservice has its own deployment pipeline, meaning that teams can work on different

services concurrently.

7. **Fault Isolation**: Since microservices are loosely coupled and independently deployed, failure in one service doesn't necessarily impact the others. If the product search service in an e-commerce system fails, the checkout and payment systems might continue to operate unaffected. This isolation contributes to the overall resilience of the application.

8. **Scalability**: One of the most compelling reasons to adopt microservices is scalability. Since each service is deployed independently, it can be scaled horizontally to meet demand. For example, if user authentication experiences heavy traffic, you can scale only that service without affecting others. This makes microservices ideal for applications with varying load patterns.

In summary, microservices are a flexible, scalable, and maintainable approach to software development, allowing teams to work on individual services that together form a cohesive application. By decomposing an application into discrete, manageable services, organizations can innovate faster and handle changes with less risk.

Serverless: Breaking Down the Concept

Serverless computing has revolutionized the way applications are deployed and managed. The term "serverless" is somewhat misleading because servers still exist; however, the responsibility for managing those servers is abstracted away from the developer and handled entirely by the cloud provider. The key to serverless is that developers no longer need to worry about provisioning, scaling, or maintaining the underlying infrastructure. Instead, they can focus entirely on writing code, while the cloud provider takes care of everything else.

The most common implementation of serverless architecture is **Function as a Service (FaaS)**, where developers write small, self-contained functions that are triggered by specific events (e.g., HTTP requests, database updates, file uploads). These functions run in stateless compute containers, are ephemeral (lasting only for the duration of the task), and scale automatically based on the number of incoming events.

Key characteristics of serverless computing include:

1. **No Infrastructure Management**: In a traditional setup, developers need to manage servers, virtual machines, or containers, ensuring that the right amount of resources are available at any given time. With serverless, the cloud provider manages all of this. The developer simply uploads their code, and the cloud provider handles everything else, from provisioning resources to scaling based on demand.

2. **Event-Driven Execution**: Serverless functions are triggered by events. These events can come from various sources, such as HTTP requests (via an API Gateway), database changes, messages in a queue, or even scheduled tasks. The function executes only when the event occurs, making it a cost-effective solution since you're only charged for the time the function runs.

3. **Auto-Scaling**: One of the most attractive features of serverless is its ability to automatically scale based on demand. If an application receives a surge in traffic, the serverless platform will automatically spin up more function instances to handle the load. When the traffic subsides, the platform reduces the number of instances accordingly.

4. **Pay-as-You-Go Pricing**: In traditional architectures, you pay for servers or virtual machines regardless of how much they are being used. With serverless, you only pay for the actual time your functions are running. This means that if your function runs for only a few milliseconds, you only pay for those milliseconds, making it a highly cost-effective solution for many use cases.

5. **Ephemeral Functions**: Serverless functions are stateless and short-lived. Once a function completes its task, it terminates, and no resources are consumed until the function is invoked again. This stateless nature allows serverless applications to be highly scalable and resilient.

6. **Built-In High Availability**: Most serverless platforms come with built-in high availability and fault tolerance. Since the infrastructure is

managed by the cloud provider, it is spread across multiple data centers or regions, ensuring that applications remain available even if part of the infrastructure fails.

7. **Focus on Business Logic**: Serverless abstracts away the operational overhead, allowing developers to focus on writing code and building features. This frees up valuable development time and resources that would otherwise be spent managing infrastructure.

Serverless architecture is most commonly associated with **Function as a Service (FaaS)**, but it also includes other managed services that work seamlessly with FaaS to build entire applications. For example, a serverless application might use managed databases (such as AWS DynamoDB or Azure Cosmos DB), serverless queues (such as Amazon SQS), and storage solutions (like AWS S3) to create a fully serverless architecture without ever needing to manage a server.

In short, serverless computing is a cloud-native model that abstracts away infrastructure management, allowing developers to focus solely on building and deploying applications.

Microservices and Serverless: A Paradigm Shift

The combination of microservices and serverless architectures represents a profound shift in how modern applications are built and deployed. Each approach introduces unique advantages, but together they create a highly scalable, cost-efficient, and maintainable solution that allows teams to innovate rapidly.

1. **Independence and Decoupling**: Microservices architecture promotes the idea that each service should operate independently of others. Serverless takes this concept a step further by allowing each microservice to be implemented as a function or set of functions. Each function can be triggered by an event and can be scaled independently, allowing for a truly decoupled system where individual services can evolve without

impacting the rest of the application.

2. **Simplified Deployment**: In traditional microservices architectures, deploying services requires managing infrastructure, whether it's virtual machines, containers, or Kubernetes clusters. Serverless removes this operational burden. Developers can deploy microservices as functions on a serverless platform like AWS Lambda, and the platform automatically manages scaling, load balancing, and fault tolerance.

3. **Faster Development Cycles**: Microservices allow teams to work on different parts of the application in parallel, but serverless further accelerates development by removing infrastructure management from the equation. Developers can focus entirely on writing code for individual services, leaving deployment and scaling to the serverless platform.

4. **Event-Driven Design**: Microservices are often designed around domain-driven principles, where different parts of the application represent specific business functions. These functions are naturally event-driven. For example, when a user submits a purchase, an event is triggered that activates the payment service, inventory service, and notification service. Serverless fits seamlessly into this event-driven model, allowing services to respond to real-time events efficiently.

5. **Cost Efficiency**: Microservices allow individual components of an application to scale independently, but serverless optimizes costs even further by only charging for actual function execution time. This pay-as-you-go model is ideal for microservices, where different services may experience varying levels of traffic. For example, a service responsible for generating monthly reports might run infrequently, while an authentication service might handle thousands of requests per second. Serverless allows you to scale both services independently while paying only for the resources they actually use.

6. **Resilience and Fault Tolerance**: Both microservices and serverless architectures emphasize fault tolerance. In a microservices architecture, failure in one service does not necessarily impact others. Serverless platforms enhance this resilience by providing built-in redundancy

and automatic failover for functions. If a function fails, the platform automatically retries the operation or triggers fallback mechanisms, ensuring high availability and resilience.

This paradigm shift to microservices and serverless has changed how organizations build and maintain applications. Instead of dealing with the complexities of scaling monolithic systems, teams can now focus on building highly modular, scalable, and maintainable solutions.

Benefits and Challenges of Microservices in Serverless

Benefits:

1. **Cost Optimization**:

- One of the biggest advantages of combining microservices with serverless is cost optimization. With traditional server-based architectures, you must provision resources that run 24/7, even if they are not fully utilized. Serverless eliminates this waste by charging only for actual usage, allowing businesses to optimize costs, especially for microservices that experience fluctuating demand.

1. **Scalability**:

- Serverless platforms automatically scale individual microservices based on incoming events. This dynamic scaling ensures that services can handle traffic spikes without manual intervention or complex autoscaling configurations. For example, if a promotional event generates high traffic to a product catalog service, the serverless platform automatically scales the function to meet demand, then scales down when traffic decreases.

1. **Simplified Operations**:

- By offloading infrastructure management to the cloud provider, teams can focus on building features and delivering value to customers. This simplicity extends to deployment, scaling, and monitoring, all of which are handled automatically by the serverless platform. As a result, DevOps teams can spend less time managing infrastructure and more time improving the application.

1. **Fault Isolation**:

- In a microservices architecture, each service is isolated from others, meaning a failure in one service doesn't impact the entire system. Serverless amplifies this isolation by allowing individual functions to fail independently. If a payment processing function fails, it doesn't affect the product catalog or user authentication services.

1. **Flexibility in Development**:

- Microservices allow teams to use different programming languages, tools, and frameworks for each service. Serverless platforms support a wide range of languages, allowing teams to choose the best tool for the job. For example, a machine learning service might be built in Python, while a high-performance API might be written in Go.

Challenges:

1. **Cold Starts**:

- One of the challenges of serverless is **cold starts**—the delay that occurs when a serverless function is invoked after a period of inactivity. This can cause performance issues for latency-sensitive applications. Although serverless platforms are constantly improving cold start times, it remains a consideration for developers when designing real-time services.

1. **Monitoring and Debugging**:

- While serverless simplifies many aspects of operations, monitoring and debugging serverless microservices can be more complex than traditional architectures. Since functions are stateless and ephemeral, developers need to rely on external tools for logging, monitoring, and tracing. Tools like AWS X-Ray, Azure Monitor, and Google Stackdriver can help, but developers must design their functions with observability in mind.

1. **State Management**:

- Serverless functions are stateless by nature, which means they don't maintain any persistent state between invocations. This presents challenges for applications that require state management. Developers must use external services, such as managed databases (e.g., DynamoDB or Firestore) or caching systems (e.g., Redis) to maintain state across function invocations.

1. **Vendor Lock-In**:

- While serverless platforms offer many advantages, they often tie you to a specific cloud provider's ecosystem. For example, an application built on AWS Lambda might rely heavily on other AWS services, making it difficult to migrate to another platform without significant refactoring.

1. **Complexity of Microservices**:

- While microservices provide flexibility and scalability, they also introduce complexity, especially in terms of service coordination, API management, and data consistency. Developers must be mindful of these challenges and implement strategies like service discovery, centralized logging, and distributed tracing to maintain operational efficiency.

Overview of Popular Serverless Platforms (AWS, Azure, GCP)

There are several popular serverless platforms available today, with **Amazon Web Services (AWS)**, **Microsoft Azure**, and **Google Cloud Platform (GCP)** leading the way. Each platform provides its own unique set of tools and services for building serverless applications, but they all share the same core principles of event-driven execution, automatic scaling, and pay-as-you-go pricing.

1. **AWS Lambda (Amazon Web Services)**

AWS Lambda is one of the most widely used serverless platforms and was among the first to popularize serverless computing. Lambda allows developers to run code in response to various triggers, such as HTTP requests (via Amazon API Gateway), database changes (via Amazon DynamoDB), and messages (via Amazon SQS).

Key features of AWS Lambda include:

- **Supports Multiple Languages**: AWS Lambda supports a variety of programming languages, including Node.js, Python, Java, Go, Ruby, and .NET Core. This flexibility allows teams to choose the best language for their specific use case.
- **Event Sources**: Lambda can be triggered by a wide range of AWS services, making it highly integrated with the AWS ecosystem. Common triggers include changes to Amazon S3 (object storage), DynamoDB (NoSQL database), and SNS (Simple Notification Service).
- **Pay-per-Invocation Pricing**: AWS Lambda uses a pay-as-you-go pricing model, charging based on the number of function invocations and the duration of each invocation. This makes it a cost-effective solution for applications with varying traffic patterns.
- **AWS Step Functions**: Lambda integrates with AWS Step Functions, which allows developers to orchestrate complex workflows across multiple Lambda functions. This is particularly useful for implementing serverless microservices that require coordination between services.

19

2. Azure Functions (Microsoft Azure)

Azure Functions is Microsoft's serverless computing platform, offering similar functionality to AWS Lambda. Azure Functions is part of the broader Azure cloud ecosystem and provides seamless integration with other Azure services like Cosmos DB, Event Grid, and Service Bus.

Key features of Azure Functions include:

- **Supports Multiple Languages**: Azure Functions supports multiple programming languages, including C#, F#, JavaScript, Python, and Java. It also allows developers to run custom code in any language using the custom handler feature.
- **Integration with Azure Services**: Azure Functions integrates deeply with Azure services, allowing developers to trigger functions based on events from Azure Cosmos DB (NoSQL database), Azure Event Grid (event routing), and Azure Storage.
- **Durable Functions**: Azure offers a feature called **Durable Functions**, which allows developers to write stateful workflows in a serverless environment. This is particularly useful for implementing long-running workflows or coordinating multiple serverless functions in a microservices architecture.
- **Pay-per-Use Pricing**: Similar to AWS Lambda, Azure Functions uses a pay-per-use pricing model, charging for function invocations and execution time. This model provides cost efficiency for applications that don't require constant uptime.

3. Google Cloud Functions (Google Cloud Platform)

Google Cloud Functions is Google's serverless platform, offering a simple way to run code in response to events from other Google Cloud services, such as Google Cloud Storage, Firebase, and Pub/Sub.

Key features of Google Cloud Functions include:

- **Supports Multiple Languages**: Google Cloud Functions supports several programming languages, including Node.js, Python, Go, and

Java, allowing developers to build serverless applications in the language of their choice.

- **Firebase Integration**: Google Cloud Functions is tightly integrated with Firebase, Google's mobile and web application development platform. This makes it a popular choice for developers building serverless applications for mobile and web apps.

- **Event-Driven Architecture**: Google Cloud Functions can be triggered by events from Google Cloud services, such as changes in Google Cloud Storage (object storage), Firestore (NoSQL database), and Pub/Sub (messaging service).

- **Simple Pricing Model**: Google Cloud Functions uses a straightforward pricing model, charging based on function invocations and execution time. This makes it a cost-effective solution for building event-driven microservices.

Conclusion

Microservices and serverless architectures represent a transformative approach to building modern, scalable applications. By combining the modularity and independence of microservices with the efficiency and scalability of serverless platforms, organizations can build applications that are more resilient, cost-effective, and easier to manage than ever before.

Each of the popular serverless platforms—AWS Lambda, Azure Functions, and Google Cloud Functions—offers unique features and integrations that make them well-suited for implementing serverless microservices. By understanding the strengths and challenges of each platform, developers can make informed decisions about how to design and deploy their applications in the cloud.

In the following chapters, we will explore specific design patterns, real-world use cases, and best practices for building microservices on serverless platforms. Through these patterns and examples, you'll gain the tools and knowledge needed to build scalable, maintainable, and cost-efficient serverless microservices.

Chapter 2: Core Principles of Microservices Design for Serverless Applications

I n this chapter, we will explore the fundamental principles that guide the design of microservices for serverless applications. These principles help ensure that applications built using microservices and serverless architecture remain scalable, maintainable, and flexible. We will cover the concepts of decoupling services for flexibility, stateless vs. stateful services, the single responsibility principle, loose coupling, and best practices for scalable microservices design.

Decoupling Services for Flexibility

Decoupling services is one of the foundational principles of microservices architecture. In a decoupled architecture, each microservice is designed to be independent of other services, allowing them to evolve, scale, and be deployed separately. This flexibility is a major advantage over traditional monolithic architectures, where changes to one part of the system can affect the entire application.

Why Decoupling Matters

Decoupling services promotes modularity, allowing different teams to work on different parts of the system simultaneously without stepping on each other's toes. By reducing dependencies between services, decoupling also reduces the risk that a failure in one service will cause cascading failures throughout the system. In a serverless architecture, decoupling allows each function or service to scale independently based on demand, optimizing resource usage and ensuring that the system remains responsive under varying workloads.

For example, in an e-commerce platform, decoupling the product catalog, payment processing, and order management services allows each of these services to scale independently based on demand. If the product catalog experiences a surge in traffic due to a marketing promotion, it can scale without affecting the payment processing service, which may have lower traffic at that time.

Techniques for Decoupling Services

There are several techniques that can be used to decouple services in a microservices architecture:

1. **Use of APIs for Communication**: Each service should expose a well-defined API that other services can interact with. This ensures that the internal implementation of each service is hidden from the rest of the system. For example, a payment service might expose APIs for initiating payments, checking payment status, and refunding transactions. Other services, such as the order management service, can call these APIs without needing to know how the payment service is implemented.

2. **Asynchronous Communication**: Decoupling can be further enhanced by using asynchronous communication patterns, such as message queues or event streams. In asynchronous communication, services send messages or events to a message broker or event bus, and other services consume those messages or events. This allows services to operate independently of each other's availability or response times. For instance, when an order is placed, the order management service could publish an event to a message queue, and the payment service would consume the event and process the payment.

3. **Event-Driven Architecture**: Event-driven architecture is a natural fit

for serverless and microservices systems. In an event-driven system, services respond to events, which are typically generated by user actions or changes in the system state. For example, when a user completes a purchase, an event is generated that triggers a series of actions across multiple microservices, such as updating the inventory, processing the payment, and sending a confirmation email. Event-driven systems allow for loose coupling between services and are well-suited for dynamic, scalable applications.

4. **Service Discovery**: In a microservices architecture, services often need to communicate with each other dynamically. Service discovery is a technique that allows services to find each other based on a service registry. This removes the need for hard-coded dependencies between services. In a serverless architecture, service discovery is less critical because many services communicate through APIs or event-based systems, but it can still be useful for certain use cases.

Decoupling services for flexibility is a critical principle in microservices design. By reducing dependencies between services, you can build systems that are more resilient, scalable, and easier to maintain. This is especially important in a serverless environment, where services need to scale independently and be highly responsive to changing workloads.

Stateless vs. Stateful Services in Serverless

In a serverless architecture, the distinction between stateless and stateful services plays a crucial role in how you design your microservices. Understanding the difference between these two concepts is essential for building scalable, resilient, and efficient applications.

Stateless Services

Stateless services are services that do not retain any state or information between requests. Each request to a stateless service is treated independently, meaning that the service does not rely on any previous interactions to fulfill the request. In serverless architecture, functions such as AWS Lambda or

Azure Functions are inherently stateless by design.

Key Characteristics of Stateless Services:

- **No Persistent State**: Stateless services do not store any data or context between invocations. Any information needed to process a request must be passed in as part of the request itself, or retrieved from an external source (e.g., a database).
- **Scalability**: Stateless services are highly scalable because each request can be handled independently. This allows serverless platforms to scale stateless services horizontally without worrying about how to maintain state across different instances.
- **Simplicity**: Stateless services are easier to manage because they don't have to deal with issues related to session management, data synchronization, or consistency between different instances.

For example, a stateless microservice in an e-commerce system could be responsible for generating product recommendations based on user behavior. The service doesn't need to remember the user's previous interactions; instead, it queries a database for relevant information and generates recommendations on the fly.

Stateful Services

Stateful services, on the other hand, retain some form of state or context between requests. This state can be user sessions, application state, or data that is used to process future requests. In traditional architectures, stateful services are common, as many applications rely on maintaining user sessions, keeping track of transactions, or storing intermediate results.

However, in serverless environments, designing stateful services can be challenging because serverless functions are inherently stateless. To handle state in serverless applications, developers must use external services such as databases, caches, or distributed storage systems.

Key Characteristics of Stateful Services:

- **Retain State Across Requests**: Stateful services need to maintain data

25

or context between different requests. This can be done using session data, distributed caches, or persistent storage.

- **Harder to Scale**: Stateful services are more challenging to scale because the state needs to be managed across multiple instances. For example, if a stateful service is scaled across multiple servers, the state needs to be shared or synchronized between those servers, which can introduce complexity.
- **Increased Complexity**: Maintaining state adds complexity to a service. You must handle issues like data consistency, concurrency, and potential failures in a more sophisticated way.

An example of a stateful service in an e-commerce platform could be a shopping cart service. The shopping cart needs to remember the items a user has added, even as the user navigates through different parts of the website. In a serverless architecture, this state might be stored in a database or a cache like Redis, with each request updating the stored state as necessary.

Managing State in Serverless Architectures

Since serverless functions are stateless, handling state in a serverless architecture requires using external storage systems. Some of the most common approaches to managing state in serverless architectures include:

1. **Database Storage**: For persistent state, serverless applications can store data in a database. Managed databases like AWS DynamoDB, Azure Cosmos DB, or Google Firestore are ideal for serverless environments because they are scalable, highly available, and don't require any infrastructure management. For example, a user session could be stored in DynamoDB, and each time the user interacts with the application, the serverless function retrieves and updates the session data in the database.

2. **Caching**: For temporary or frequently accessed data, caching systems like Redis or Memcached can be used to store state. These systems provide low-latency access to data, making them ideal for applications that require fast state retrieval, such as real-time analytics or recommen-

dation engines.

3. **Session Management**: In applications where user sessions need to be maintained, a distributed session management solution can be used. This might involve storing session data in a database, or using tokens like JWT (JSON Web Token) to maintain session state on the client side.

4. **Stateful Services with Event Sourcing**: In event-driven architectures, state can be managed by using an event-sourcing approach. Instead of storing the current state of an entity, event sourcing stores a sequence of events that describe changes to the entity over time. By replaying these events, the current state can be reconstructed. This approach is often used in conjunction with message queues or event streams.

By understanding the trade-offs between stateless and stateful services, developers can design microservices that are optimized for serverless environments. Stateless services offer simplicity and scalability, while stateful services require more careful consideration of how to store and manage state outside the serverless function.

Single Responsibility Principle

The **Single Responsibility Principle (SRP)** is one of the key principles in microservices design, and it plays an important role in ensuring that services are maintainable and scalable. The Single Responsibility Principle states that a service should have only one reason to change. In other words, a microservice should be responsible for only one specific business function or domain.

By adhering to SRP, developers can create microservices that are highly focused and modular. This modularity makes it easier to manage, test, and scale individual services. For example, if a microservice is responsible for processing payments, it should only handle tasks related to payments (e.g., initiating transactions, processing refunds, and verifying payment status). Other tasks, such as managing customer profiles or handling shipping, should be handled by separate microservices.

Benefits of the Single Responsibility Principle

1. **Maintainability**: When each microservice has a single responsibility, it becomes easier to maintain and update. Changes to a specific business function can be made without affecting other parts of the system. For example, if you need to add support for a new payment provider, you can make the change in the payment service without touching the order or inventory services.

2. **Scalability**: Services that adhere to SRP can be scaled independently. For instance, if the payment service experiences high traffic during peak hours, it can be scaled up without impacting other services. This makes the system more efficient and reduces resource consumption.

3. **Testability**: Microservices with a single responsibility are easier to test because they have a clear and well-defined scope. Unit tests and integration tests can focus on specific functionality, ensuring that each service behaves as expected.

4. **Fault Isolation**: When services are designed with a single responsibility, failures in one service are less likely to affect other services. For example, if the payment service encounters an error, the rest of the system (e.g., product catalog or order management) can continue to operate.

Applying the Single Responsibility Principle in Serverless Microservices

In serverless architectures, the Single Responsibility Principle is especially important because serverless functions are designed to be lightweight and short-lived. By ensuring that each function is focused on a single responsibility, developers can create efficient, scalable serverless microservices.

For example, consider a serverless e-commerce application. Instead of having a single function handle the entire order process, you can break it down into multiple functions, each with a single responsibility:

- **Order Creation Function**: This function is responsible for creating new orders and adding them to the order management system.
- **Payment Processing Function**: This function handles the payment

transaction for the order, interacting with external payment gateways as needed.

- **Shipping Function**: This function updates the shipping status of the order and sends notifications to the customer.

Each of these functions has a single responsibility, making the system more modular and easier to manage. If the payment processing function needs to be updated, the other functions remain unaffected, reducing the risk of introducing bugs or performance issues.

By adhering to the Single Responsibility Principle, developers can create serverless microservices that are easier to maintain, scale, and test.

The Importance of Loose Coupling

Loose coupling is a design principle that emphasizes minimizing dependencies between services or components. In a loosely coupled system, each service has little or no knowledge of the internal workings of other services. This allows services to evolve independently and reduces the risk of cascading failures when one service experiences issues.

In a microservices architecture, loose coupling is achieved by ensuring that services communicate through well-defined APIs and do not rely on shared resources or internal details of other services. Loose coupling is particularly important in serverless architectures, where services need to scale independently and respond to events in real-time.

Why Loose Coupling Matters

1. **Flexibility and Agility**: Loosely coupled services can be updated or replaced without affecting the rest of the system. This allows teams to iterate faster and release new features more frequently. For example, if you need to update the payment gateway used by your payment service, you can make the change without impacting the other services in your system.

2. **Fault Tolerance**: Loose coupling reduces the risk that a failure in one

service will propagate to other services. For example, if the inventory service goes down, the order management service should still be able to process orders and queue them for fulfillment once the inventory service is back online.

3. **Scalability**: Services that are loosely coupled can be scaled independently based on demand. For example, the user authentication service might experience a high volume of traffic during peak hours, while the product catalog service might experience more consistent traffic throughout the day. By decoupling these services, you can scale them independently to meet demand.

4. **Maintainability**: Loosely coupled systems are easier to maintain because each service can be updated, tested, and deployed independently. This reduces the risk of introducing bugs when making changes to the system.

Techniques for Achieving Loose Coupling

1. **API-Driven Design**: One of the most effective ways to achieve loose coupling is through API-driven design. Each service should expose a well-defined API that other services can interact with. This API acts as a contract between services, ensuring that services can communicate without needing to know the internal details of each other.

2. **Message-Based Communication**: In a serverless microservices architecture, message-based communication is an effective way to achieve loose coupling. Services can send messages or events to a message broker or event bus (such as AWS SNS, AWS SQS, or Apache Kafka), and other services can consume those messages asynchronously. This decouples the services and allows them to operate independently of each other's availability or response times.

3. **Event-Driven Architecture**: Event-driven architecture is another technique for achieving loose coupling. In an event-driven system, services respond to events rather than making direct calls to other services. For example, when an order is placed, the order management

service publishes an event to an event bus, and the payment service consumes the event and processes the payment. This decouples the order management service from the payment service, allowing them to evolve independently.

4. **Avoiding Shared Databases**: In a loosely coupled system, each service should have its own database or data store. Sharing databases between services can create tight coupling, as changes to the schema or data structure can affect multiple services. By giving each service its own database, you can ensure that services are isolated from each other's data models.

Loose coupling is a critical principle in microservices design, especially in serverless architectures. By minimizing dependencies between services, you can build systems that are more resilient, scalable, and easier to maintain.

Best Practices for Designing Scalable Microservices

Designing scalable microservices requires careful consideration of several factors, including how services communicate, how they handle failures, and how they scale based on demand. In this section, we will explore best practices for designing microservices that can scale effectively in a serverless architecture.

1. **Design for Scalability from the Start**

One of the key advantages of microservices is their ability to scale independently. However, to fully leverage this advantage, it's important to design your services with scalability in mind from the start. This means thinking about how each service will handle increased traffic, how it will interact with other services, and how it will store and manage data.

In a serverless architecture, scalability is largely handled by the platform itself. Serverless platforms automatically scale functions based on demand, ensuring that your services can handle traffic spikes without manual intervention. However, you still need to design your services in a way that takes advantage of this scalability.

Key Considerations for Scalability:

- **Statelessness**: Stateless services are easier to scale because each request can be handled independently. By keeping your services stateless, you allow the serverless platform to scale them horizontally without worrying about maintaining session state or synchronizing data between instances.
- **Asynchronous Communication**: Asynchronous communication patterns, such as message queues or event streams, can help your services scale more effectively. Instead of making synchronous API calls, services can publish messages to a message broker, allowing other services to consume them at their own pace. This decouples services and allows them to scale independently.
- **Caching**: Implement caching to reduce the load on your services and improve response times. For example, if a service frequently queries a database for the same information, you can use a caching layer (such as Redis or a CDN) to store the results of those queries and serve them more quickly.

2. Implement Resilience and Fault Tolerance

In a distributed system like microservices, failures are inevitable. To ensure that your services remain available and responsive in the face of failures, it's important to design them with resilience and fault tolerance in mind.

Key Techniques for Fault Tolerance:

- **Retry Mechanisms**: Implement retry mechanisms for failed requests or operations. For example, if a service call fails due to a temporary network issue, the service should automatically retry the operation after a short delay. Serverless platforms often provide built-in support for retries.
- **Circuit Breakers**: Circuit breakers are a pattern used to prevent a failing service from overloading the system. If a service repeatedly fails, the circuit breaker will open, preventing further requests from reaching the service until it recovers. This helps prevent cascading failures in a microservices architecture.

- **Timeouts**: Set timeouts for service calls to avoid long-running operations that could degrade system performance. For example, if a service does not respond within a certain time frame, the request should be terminated, and a fallback mechanism should be triggered.

3. Optimize for Cost Efficiency

One of the major advantages of serverless architecture is its cost efficiency. Serverless platforms use a pay-as-you-go pricing model, meaning you only pay for the time your functions are running. However, to fully optimize for cost efficiency, it's important to design your services in a way that minimizes unnecessary resource consumption.

Key Techniques for Cost Optimization:

- **Function Consolidation**: Avoid creating too many small functions that are invoked frequently. Instead, consolidate related functionality into fewer functions to reduce the overhead of invoking multiple functions.
- **Efficient Data Storage**: Use efficient data storage mechanisms, such as NoSQL databases, to reduce the cost of storing and retrieving data. For example, AWS DynamoDB offers on-demand capacity pricing, which automatically adjusts based on your actual usage.
- **Monitor and Optimize**: Use monitoring tools to track the performance and cost of your serverless functions. For example, AWS CloudWatch can provide insights into how your functions are being used and help you identify areas where you can optimize performance and reduce costs.

4. Use Observability and Monitoring

Monitoring and observability are critical for ensuring that your microservices are operating as expected. In a

4o

ChatGPT said:

ChatGPT

serverless architecture, it can be challenging to understand the health and performance of individual functions, so implementing robust monitoring practices is essential.

Key Observability Practices:

- **Centralized Logging**: Use centralized logging solutions to collect and analyze logs from your serverless functions. This allows you to identify issues and monitor performance across multiple services.
- **Distributed Tracing**: Implement distributed tracing to gain visibility into the flow of requests across your microservices. Tools like AWS X-Ray, OpenTelemetry, and Zipkin can help you trace requests as they move through different services and identify bottlenecks or failures.
- **Performance Metrics**: Track key performance metrics, such as response times, error rates, and throughput, for each of your services. Monitoring these metrics allows you to proactively identify issues and ensure that your services remain responsive and reliable.

5. Implement Security Best Practices

Security is a critical consideration in microservices design, especially in a serverless architecture where services often communicate over public networks. Implementing security best practices is essential for protecting sensitive data and ensuring the integrity of your application.

Key Security Practices:

- **Authentication and Authorization**: Implement strong authentication and authorization mechanisms for your APIs. Use industry-standard protocols like OAuth2 or OpenID Connect to secure access to your services.
- **Data Encryption**: Encrypt sensitive data both in transit and at rest. Use TLS/SSL to secure communication between services and encrypt data stored in databases or storage systems.
- **Network Security**: Use virtual private clouds (VPCs) and security groups to control network access to your serverless functions. Limit access to only those services and users that require it.

By following these best practices for designing scalable microservices, developers can create resilient, efficient, and secure applications that take full advantage of the benefits of serverless architecture. The principles of decoupling, statelessness, single responsibility, loose coupling, and observability all contribute to building successful microservices that can thrive in a serverless environment.

Conclusion

In this chapter, we explored the core principles of microservices design for serverless applications. By focusing on decoupling services for flexibility, understanding the differences between stateless and stateful services, adhering to the Single Responsibility Principle, prioritizing loose coupling, and implementing best practices for scalability, developers can create robust and efficient microservices that leverage the strengths of serverless architecture.

As we continue our exploration of microservices and serverless computing, we will delve deeper into design patterns, strategies, and real-world use cases that illustrate how these principles come together to create modern applications that are ready to meet the demands of today's digital landscape.

Chapter 3: Event-Driven Architecture and Asynchronous Communication

E vent-driven architecture (EDA) is a powerful paradigm for designing microservices that are responsive, scalable, and decoupled. This chapter will delve into the concepts of event-driven microservices, various design patterns such as publisher-subscriber, event sourcing, and CQRS (Command Query Responsibility Segregation), and how asynchronous communication can be implemented in serverless environments. Additionally, we will explore a case study using AWS Lambda with Amazon SNS (Simple Notification Service) and SQS (Simple Queue Service) to demonstrate the practical applications of these concepts, as well as the pros and cons of event-driven design in serverless applications.

Understanding Event-Driven Microservices

Event-driven microservices are designed to react to events—significant occurrences or changes in state—within the system. In this architecture, services communicate primarily through events, allowing for loose coupling and improved scalability. Rather than relying on synchronous calls between services, event-driven microservices listen for events and take action when those events occur.

Key Concepts of Event-Driven Architecture

1. **Events**: An event represents a change in state or an occurrence within a system. For instance, a user placing an order, a payment being processed, or an inventory item being updated can all be considered events. In an event-driven architecture, these events are the primary means of communication between services.

2. **Producers and Consumers**: In an event-driven system, services can act as both producers and consumers of events. A producer generates an event and publishes it to a message broker or event bus, while a consumer listens for and reacts to events. This allows for flexible communication patterns where services can interact without direct knowledge of each other.

3. **Event Brokers**: An event broker is a middleware component that facilitates the communication of events between producers and consumers. It acts as an intermediary that decouples the services, allowing them to operate independently. Common event brokers include Apache Kafka, RabbitMQ, AWS SNS, and Azure Event Grid.

4. **Asynchronous Communication**: In an event-driven architecture, services communicate asynchronously. This means that when a service publishes an event, it does not wait for a response from the consumers. Instead, it continues processing other tasks, allowing for improved performance and responsiveness.

5. **Loose Coupling**: One of the main advantages of event-driven architecture is the loose coupling it provides between services. Since services communicate through events rather than direct calls, they can evolve independently. Changes made to one service do not require changes to others, promoting a more flexible and maintainable architecture.

Patterns: Publisher-Subscriber, Event Sourcing, and CQRS

In event-driven architecture, several patterns are commonly used to manage the flow of events and data between services. Three prominent patterns are the publisher-subscriber pattern, event sourcing, and CQRS.

1. Publisher-Subscriber Pattern

The publisher-subscriber (pub-sub) pattern is a messaging pattern where producers (publishers) send messages to a central broker, which then distributes those messages to multiple consumers (subscribers) that are interested in the events.

- **How It Works**: In a pub-sub system, a publisher publishes events to a topic in the message broker. Subscribers express interest in specific topics, and when an event is published to that topic, the broker delivers the event to all interested subscribers.
- **Use Case**: A common use case for the pub-sub pattern is in real-time applications, such as chat applications or social media platforms, where multiple consumers need to receive updates about new messages, posts, or notifications. For example, when a user posts a new message, the message can be published to a topic, and all users subscribed to that topic receive the update.
- **Advantages**: The pub-sub pattern decouples publishers and subscribers, allowing them to evolve independently. It also enables scalability, as new subscribers can be added without modifying the publisher.

2. Event Sourcing

Event sourcing is a pattern where the state of an application is derived from a sequence of events rather than being stored in a traditional database. Instead of persisting the current state, all changes to the state are stored as a series of events.

- **How It Works**: In an event-sourced system, each action taken by the user is recorded as an event in the order it occurred. To reconstruct the current state of the application, the system replays all the events from the beginning. For example, if a user updates their profile, the change is recorded as an event (e.g., "Profile Updated") rather than directly modifying the profile data in a database.
- **Use Case**: Event sourcing is particularly useful in applications that require an audit trail, history of changes, or complex business logic that

depends on past actions. For example, in a banking application, event sourcing can be used to track transactions and maintain an accurate history of account balances.

- **Advantages**: Event sourcing provides a complete history of changes, allowing for easy auditing and debugging. It also enables rebuilding the state of the application at any point in time and can improve performance by allowing efficient storage and retrieval of state changes.

3. CQRS (Command Query Responsibility Segregation)

CQRS is a pattern that separates the handling of commands (write operations) and queries (read operations) into distinct models. This separation allows for optimized designs for each use case, improving performance and scalability.

- **How It Works**: In a CQRS architecture, commands are responsible for modifying the state of the application, while queries are used to retrieve data. For example, in an e-commerce application, the order service might have separate command handlers for placing orders and updating inventory, while query handlers are responsible for retrieving order history or product details.
- **Use Case**: CQRS is particularly beneficial in complex domains where read and write operations have different performance and scaling requirements. For example, in a high-traffic application where reads vastly outnumber writes, using separate models for reading and writing can optimize performance.
- **Advantages**: CQRS allows for the optimization of the data models used for reads and writes, leading to improved performance. It also enables better separation of concerns, making it easier to manage complex business logic.

Implementing Asynchronous Communication in Serverless

Asynchronous communication is a key aspect of event-driven architecture and is particularly well-suited for serverless applications. In serverless environments, implementing asynchronous communication can help improve scalability, responsiveness, and resilience.

Techniques for Asynchronous Communication

1. **Message Queues**: Message queues allow services to communicate asynchronously by sending messages to a queue that other services can consume. AWS SQS (Simple Queue Service) is a widely used managed message queuing service that can be easily integrated into serverless applications. When a service needs to communicate an event or task, it sends a message to the queue, and other services can poll the queue to retrieve messages when they are ready to process them.

- **Benefits**: Message queues decouple the services and provide reliability. If a service is unavailable or busy, messages can be stored in the queue until the service is ready to process them.

1. **Event Streams**: Event streams allow for the continuous flow of events, enabling real-time processing of data. AWS Kinesis and Apache Kafka are popular platforms for managing event streams. Services can publish events to the stream, and other services can consume the events as they occur.

- **Benefits**: Event streams provide a scalable and efficient way to handle large volumes of events in real-time. They enable powerful analytics and monitoring capabilities by allowing services to process data in motion.

1. **Pub-Sub Systems**: The pub-sub pattern can be implemented using managed services like AWS SNS (Simple Notification Service) or Google Cloud Pub/Sub. In this setup, publishers send messages to a topic, and

subscribers listen for those messages. This allows for easy integration between multiple services.

- **Benefits**: Pub-sub systems enable decoupled communication and allow for multiple subscribers to receive the same events without impacting the producer's performance.

1. **Webhooks**: Webhooks provide a way for services to receive real-time notifications of events. When an event occurs in one service, it sends an HTTP request (webhook) to another service, notifying it of the change. This is commonly used in integrations between third-party services.

- **Benefits**: Webhooks allow for real-time communication without requiring the consumer to poll for updates. They are simple to implement and can be easily integrated into existing workflows.

Case Study: Using AWS Lambda with SNS and SQS

To illustrate the concepts of event-driven architecture and asynchronous communication in serverless applications, let's explore a case study involving AWS Lambda, SNS, and SQS.

Scenario

Consider an e-commerce application that needs to process orders, manage inventory, and send notifications to customers. The application requires an event-driven architecture to handle the different tasks associated with order processing while ensuring scalability and responsiveness.

Architecture Overview

1. **Order Service**: When a customer places an order, the order service creates an order record and publishes an event to an SNS topic (e.g., "OrderPlaced"). This event contains relevant details about the order, such as the order ID and customer information.
2. **Inventory Service**: The inventory service is subscribed to the "Or-

41

derPlaced" topic. When it receives the event, it checks the inventory levels and updates the stock accordingly. If the inventory is sufficient, it publishes an event to another SNS topic (e.g., "InventoryUpdated").

3. **Payment Service**: The payment service is also subscribed to the "OrderPlaced" topic. When it receives the event, it processes the payment for the order. If the payment is successful, it publishes an event to the "PaymentProcessed" topic.

4. **Notification Service**: The notification service listens to both the "PaymentProcessed" and "InventoryUpdated" topics. When it receives either event, it sends a confirmation email to the customer with the order details.

5. **SQS for Delayed Processing**: If either the inventory service or payment service is temporarily unavailable, the events can be sent to an SQS queue instead of being lost. The services can poll the queue and process events when they are ready, ensuring that no events are missed.

Implementation Steps

1. **Create SNS Topics**: Set up SNS topics for "OrderPlaced," "Payment-Processed," and "InventoryUpdated."

2. **Develop Lambda Functions**: Create AWS Lambda functions for the order, inventory, payment, and notification services. Each function should be configured to trigger based on events from the appropriate SNS topics.

3. **Set Up SQS Queue**: Create an SQS queue to handle delayed processing for the payment and inventory services. Configure the services to send events to the queue if they cannot process them immediately.

4. **Testing and Monitoring**: Implement logging and monitoring using AWS CloudWatch to track the performance of each Lambda function and the flow of events through the system.

Pros and Cons of Event-Driven Design in Serverless

While event-driven architecture offers many benefits, it is essential to understand the potential drawbacks as well. Below are the pros and cons of adopting event-driven design in serverless applications.

Pros

1. **Scalability**: Event-driven systems are inherently scalable. Services can scale independently based on the volume of events they need to process. Serverless platforms handle the scaling of functions automatically, ensuring that applications remain responsive under varying loads.

2. **Decoupling**: Event-driven architecture promotes loose coupling between services. Each service communicates through events, allowing them to evolve independently. This reduces the risk of cascading failures and simplifies maintenance.

3. **Asynchronous Processing**: Asynchronous communication allows services to continue processing other tasks while waiting for events. This leads to improved performance and responsiveness in applications.

4. **Real-Time Processing**: Event-driven architecture enables real-time data processing and analytics. Services can react to events as they occur, allowing for immediate updates and notifications.

5. **Fault Tolerance**: Event-driven systems are often more resilient to failures. If a service is temporarily unavailable, events can be stored and processed later, ensuring that no data is lost.

6. **Improved Resource Utilization**: By leveraging event-driven communication, resources can be utilized more efficiently. Services can scale up or down based on demand, reducing waste and optimizing costs.

Cons

1. **Complexity**: Event-driven architecture can introduce complexity in terms of design and management. Developers must carefully consider how events are generated, consumed, and processed, leading to potential

challenges in maintaining the overall system.

2. **Debugging and Monitoring**: Debugging event-driven systems can be challenging due to the asynchronous nature of communication. Tracking the flow of events across multiple services requires robust monitoring and logging tools.

3. **Event Schema Management**: Changes to the event schema can impact multiple services that rely on that schema. Managing event schemas and ensuring compatibility across services can add complexity to the system.

4. **Latency**: In some cases, event-driven systems can introduce latency, particularly if there are multiple steps in the processing pipeline. Developers must design their systems carefully to minimize delays.

5. **Learning Curve**: Developers new to event-driven architecture may face a steep learning curve. Understanding concepts such as event sourcing, pub-sub systems, and asynchronous communication requires time and practice.

Conclusion

Event-driven architecture and asynchronous communication are powerful concepts that enable the design of scalable, responsive, and decoupled microservices in serverless applications. By understanding the principles of event-driven design, developers can leverage patterns such as publisher-subscriber, event sourcing, and CQRS to build robust and efficient systems.

Implementing asynchronous communication using tools like AWS Lambda, SNS, and SQS allows teams to create responsive applications that can handle varying workloads with ease. While event-driven design offers numerous advantages, it also comes with challenges that require careful consideration and management.

In the following chapters, we will explore additional design patterns and strategies for building effective microservices on serverless platforms, further enhancing your understanding of how to leverage event-driven architecture in your applications.

Chapter 4: Designing Serverless APIs with the API Gateway Pattern

I
n today's digital landscape, APIs (Application Programming Interfaces) play a crucial role in enabling communication between different software systems. As businesses increasingly adopt serverless architectures, designing effective APIs becomes essential for building scalable and maintainable applications. This chapter explores the API Gateway pattern, its benefits, and how to implement it using popular cloud platforms like AWS and Azure. We will also cover security management, rate limiting, and common pitfalls to avoid when using API gateways in serverless environments.

Overview of the API Gateway Pattern

The API Gateway pattern is a vital architectural component in modern microservices and serverless applications. It acts as a single entry point for clients to access various backend services. Instead of exposing individual microservices directly to clients, the API gateway abstracts the complexities of service discovery, communication, and orchestration. It simplifies the interface for clients while enhancing the overall security, performance, and management of API calls.

Key Functions of an API Gateway

1. **Request Routing**: The API gateway routes incoming requests to the appropriate backend service or microservice based on the request's URL, headers, or parameters. This decouples clients from the underlying service architecture, allowing for flexibility in how services are organized.

2. **Protocol Translation**: The API gateway can handle different communication protocols (e.g., HTTP, WebSocket, gRPC) and translate between them as needed. This is especially useful in hybrid architectures where some services may use different protocols.

3. **Aggregation**: In many applications, a single client request may require data from multiple microservices. The API gateway can aggregate these requests and respond with a single, unified response. This reduces the number of round trips required between clients and services.

4. **Security**: The API gateway serves as a security layer, allowing you to enforce authentication, authorization, and access control policies before requests reach backend services. This centralizes security management and reduces the attack surface of your application.

5. **Rate Limiting and Throttling**: The API gateway can implement rate limiting and throttling policies to prevent abuse and ensure fair usage of resources. This is particularly important in public APIs, where you want to prevent excessive usage from a single client.

6. **Logging and Monitoring**: API gateways can log incoming requests, responses, and errors, providing valuable insights into the performance and usage of your APIs. Monitoring tools can be integrated to track metrics like latency, error rates, and traffic patterns.

7. **Caching**: To improve performance, the API gateway can cache responses for frequently accessed data. This reduces the load on backend services and speeds up response times for clients.

Benefits of Using an API Gateway in Serverless

Implementing an API gateway in serverless architectures offers numerous benefits that enhance both development and operational efficiency. Here are some of the primary advantages:

1. **Simplified Client Interface**: By providing a single entry point for multiple services, the API gateway simplifies the interface that clients interact with. This makes it easier for developers to integrate with the API and reduces the learning curve for new users.

2. **Decoupling of Services**: The API gateway decouples clients from the underlying services, allowing teams to modify or replace backend services without affecting client applications. This flexibility promotes agility and faster development cycles.

3. **Enhanced Security**: By centralizing security controls at the API gateway, you can implement consistent authentication and authorization policies across all services. This reduces the risk of security vulnerabilities and makes it easier to manage access control.

4. **Improved Performance**: API gateways can cache responses and reduce the number of requests sent to backend services, resulting in faster response times for clients. This is particularly beneficial for serverless applications, where cold start times can affect performance.

5. **Monitoring and Analytics**: API gateways provide built-in logging and monitoring capabilities, allowing you to track usage patterns, error rates, and performance metrics. This data can be invaluable for optimizing your APIs and identifying potential issues.

6. **Flexibility in Service Composition**: The API gateway enables developers to create composite APIs that aggregate responses from multiple services. This allows for more efficient client-server communication and can lead to a better overall user experience.

7. **Rate Limiting and Traffic Management**: API gateways provide mechanisms for implementing rate limiting, throttling, and usage quotas. This helps prevent abuse and ensures fair usage of shared resources.

Implementing the API Gateway with AWS API Gateway and Azure API Management

1. AWS API Gateway

AWS API Gateway is a fully managed service that makes it easy to create, deploy, and manage APIs at any scale. It supports RESTful APIs, WebSocket APIs, and HTTP APIs, allowing developers to choose the best option for their use cases.

Steps to Implement AWS API Gateway:

- **Create an API**: Begin by creating a new API in the AWS API Gateway console. You can choose between REST API, HTTP API, or WebSocket API based on your needs.
- **Define Resources and Methods**: Define the resources (e.g., /orders, /products) and methods (e.g., GET, POST) for your API. For each method, you can specify the integration type (Lambda function, HTTP endpoint, or AWS service).
- **Set Up Request and Response Mapping**: Configure request and response mapping templates to transform incoming requests and outgoing responses. This allows you to customize the API interface without modifying backend services.
- **Enable CORS**: If your API will be accessed from web browsers, enable Cross-Origin Resource Sharing (CORS) to allow requests from different domains.
- **Configure Security**: Implement security measures such as API keys, AWS IAM roles, or Amazon Cognito for user authentication. You can also configure resource policies to control access based on IP address or other criteria.
- **Deploy the API**: After configuring the API, deploy it to a stage (e.g., development, production). Each stage can have its own settings, including throttling and logging.
- **Monitor and Manage**: Use AWS CloudWatch to monitor API usage, track performance metrics, and set up alarms for error rates or latency

issues.

2. Azure API Management

Azure API Management (APIM) is a fully managed API gateway that enables organizations to publish, secure, transform, and analyze APIs. It provides a unified interface for managing APIs and offers built-in tools for monitoring and analytics.

Steps to Implement Azure API Management:

- **Create an API Management Instance:** Start by creating an Azure API Management instance in the Azure portal. Choose the appropriate pricing tier based on your expected usage.
- **Import or Create APIs:** You can import existing APIs from various sources (e.g., OpenAPI specifications) or create new APIs manually. Define the operations (GET, POST, etc.) for each API.
- **Set Up Policies:** Azure API Management allows you to apply policies at the global, API, or operation level. Policies can be used for various purposes, including authentication, caching, rate limiting, and transformation.
- **Enable Security:** Configure security options such as OAuth2, API keys, or Azure Active Directory (AAD) for authentication and authorization. You can also set up IP filtering and other security policies.
- **Test APIs:** Azure provides a built-in test console for testing your APIs directly within the portal. This allows you to verify functionality before deploying.
- **Monitor and Analyze:** Azure API Management integrates with Azure Monitor and Application Insights, providing valuable insights into API performance, usage patterns, and error rates.

Managing Security and Rate Limiting with the API Gateway

Security and rate limiting are critical aspects of API management, especially when exposing APIs to external clients. Here are some strategies for managing these aspects using an API gateway.

1. Security Management

- **Authentication and Authorization**: Implement strong authentication mechanisms to ensure that only authorized users can access your APIs. Common methods include:
- **API Keys**: Simple tokens that clients must include in their requests. API keys are easy to implement but may not provide robust security on their own.
- **OAuth2**: A widely used authorization framework that allows third-party applications to obtain limited access to a web service. OAuth2 is suitable for scenarios where users need to authenticate via external providers (e.g., Google, Facebook).
- **JWT (JSON Web Tokens)**: A compact token format that allows clients to authenticate and carry claims (e.g., user roles) in a single request. JWTs can be verified by the API gateway without needing to query a database.
- **Data Encryption**: Ensure that sensitive data is encrypted both in transit and at rest. Use HTTPS for all communications to protect data in transit. For data stored in databases or object storage, utilize encryption services offered by your cloud provider.
- **IP Whitelisting**: Implement IP whitelisting to restrict access to your APIs based on trusted IP addresses. This adds an additional layer of security by preventing unauthorized access from unknown sources.
- **Rate Limiting**: Use rate limiting to control the number of requests a client can make to your API within a specified time period. This helps prevent abuse and ensures fair usage among clients. Common approaches include:
- **Per-API Rate Limits**: Limit the number of requests for each API endpoint individually.

- **Client-Based Rate Limits**: Implement rate limits based on client identifiers (e.g., API keys) to manage usage across different clients.
- **Request Validation**: Implement input validation to ensure that incoming requests conform to expected formats. This helps protect against attacks such as SQL injection or cross-site scripting (XSS).

2. Rate Limiting

Rate limiting is essential for managing the consumption of API resources and ensuring fair access for all clients. Here are common strategies for implementing rate limiting with an API gateway:

- **Token Bucket Algorithm**: This algorithm allows clients to burst requests up to a defined limit while averaging the rate over time. Tokens are added to a bucket at a steady rate, and clients can make requests as long as they have tokens available. Once the bucket is empty, clients must wait until tokens are replenished.
- **Leaky Bucket Algorithm**: Similar to the token bucket, the leaky bucket algorithm allows for steady request flow while accommodating burst requests. Requests are added to a queue, and they are processed at a constant rate. If the queue fills up, excess requests are dropped.
- **Fixed Window Counter**: In this approach, a fixed time window (e.g., one minute) is defined, and a counter tracks the number of requests made by a client during that window. Once the limit is reached, any additional requests are denied until the window resets.
- **Sliding Window**: The sliding window technique maintains a count of requests over a rolling time frame. This approach provides more flexibility compared to fixed window counters, allowing clients to make requests based on their actual usage patterns.

Common Pitfalls and How to Avoid Them

While using API gateways in serverless applications provides numerous benefits, there are also potential pitfalls that developers should be aware of. Below are some common pitfalls and strategies for avoiding them:

1. Overloading the API Gateway

Pitfall: As the API gateway serves as a single entry point for multiple services, it can become a bottleneck if not properly managed. Heavy traffic can overwhelm the gateway, leading to increased latency or downtime.

Solution: Monitor traffic patterns and performance metrics to ensure the API gateway can handle the expected load. Consider implementing load balancing and scaling strategies to distribute traffic evenly across multiple instances of the API gateway.

2. Poorly Defined APIs

Pitfall: Inefficient or poorly defined APIs can lead to confusion and frustration for clients. Inconsistent naming conventions, lack of documentation, or unclear response formats can hinder developer adoption.

Solution: Use RESTful principles to define clear and consistent API endpoints. Provide comprehensive API documentation, including usage examples, response formats, and error handling guidelines. Consider using tools like Swagger/OpenAPI for automatic documentation generation.

3. Lack of Versioning

Pitfall: Failing to implement API versioning can lead to breaking changes that impact clients. As APIs evolve, changes to request and response formats can cause compatibility issues.

Solution: Implement API versioning strategies to ensure that clients can continue to use older versions while transitioning to newer ones. Common approaches include including the version number in the URL (e.g., /api/v1/resource) or using HTTP headers to specify the desired version.

4. Insufficient Monitoring and Logging

Pitfall: Without proper monitoring and logging, it can be challenging to identify issues, track performance, or troubleshoot problems. This lack of visibility can lead to prolonged downtime or degraded user experiences.

Solution: Implement robust logging and monitoring solutions for the API gateway and backend services. Use tools like AWS CloudWatch, Azure Monitor, or third-party solutions to track performance metrics, error rates, and usage patterns. Set up alerts for anomalies or performance degradation.

5. Ignoring Security Best Practices

Pitfall: Security vulnerabilities can arise if proper security measures are not implemented. This includes insufficient authentication and authorization, lack of data encryption, and inadequate input validation.

Solution: Implement comprehensive security practices, including authentication, authorization, data encryption, and input validation. Regularly review and update security policies to address emerging threats and vulnerabilities.

6. Overcomplicating the Architecture

Pitfall: Adding unnecessary complexity to the API gateway architecture can lead to challenges in maintenance and management. Overengineering can make it difficult for teams to understand and work with the system.

Solution: Keep the architecture simple and focus on core functionality. Avoid adding features or components that are not essential for meeting the requirements of your application. Regularly review and refactor the architecture as needed.

Conclusion

Designing serverless APIs using the API Gateway pattern is a powerful approach that enhances the scalability, security, and manageability of microservices. The API gateway serves as a central point for managing requests, enforcing security, and routing traffic to backend services. By leveraging platforms like AWS API Gateway and Azure API Management, developers can create robust APIs that meet the demands of modern applications.

In this chapter, we explored the API Gateway pattern, its benefits, and how to implement it using popular cloud services. We also discussed important considerations for managing security and rate limiting, as well as common pitfalls and strategies for avoiding them.

As we move forward in this book, we will continue to explore additional design patterns and best practices for building effective serverless applications, providing you with the knowledge and tools to succeed in your microservices journey.

Chapter 5: Saga Pattern for Managing Distributed Transactions

In the realm of microservices, managing distributed transactions poses a significant challenge due to the nature of independently deployed services. Traditional monolithic applications often rely on database transactions to ensure data consistency across multiple operations. However, in a microservices architecture, where services are loosely coupled and communicate over networks, ensuring data consistency across multiple services becomes complex. The **Saga Pattern** is a solution designed to address this complexity by enabling a reliable and resilient approach to managing distributed transactions.

This chapter will explore the saga pattern in depth, including its principles, implementation strategies, real-world use cases, and best practices. By understanding the saga pattern, developers can effectively manage complex workflows in microservices and ensure data integrity in their applications.

Understanding the Saga Pattern

The Saga Pattern is a design pattern that facilitates the management of distributed transactions by breaking them down into a series of smaller, independent operations (or sub-transactions) that can be executed across multiple services. Each operation in a saga is responsible for a specific part of the transaction, and if any operation fails, the saga ensures that compensating actions are taken to revert the changes made by previous operations. This approach allows for maintaining consistency in a distributed environment without relying on a single, centralized database.

Key Characteristics of the Saga Pattern

1. **Decoupled Operations**: Each operation in a saga is independent, allowing services to execute their tasks without being tightly coupled. This decoupling is essential for maintaining flexibility and scalability in microservices.
2. **Compensating Transactions**: When an operation in a saga fails, compensating transactions are triggered to undo the effects of the previous operations. This ensures that the system can return to a consistent state without requiring global locks or rollback mechanisms.
3. **Asynchronous Execution**: Sagas can operate asynchronously, allowing for parallel execution of operations. This enhances performance and reduces latency in the overall transaction process.
4. **Event-Driven Communication**: The saga pattern often utilizes event-driven architecture to coordinate the execution of operations. Events are published to indicate the completion or failure of operations, triggering subsequent actions as needed.

Types of Saga Execution

There are two primary types of saga execution: **Orchestration** and **Choreography**. Each approach has its strengths and weaknesses, and the choice between them depends on the specific requirements of the application.

1. Orchestration

In an orchestrated saga, a central coordinator (or orchestrator) is responsible for managing the flow of the saga. The orchestrator determines the sequence of operations, invokes them, and handles compensating transactions in case of failures.

- **How It Works**: The orchestrator sends requests to the involved services to perform their respective operations. After each operation, the orchestrator waits for a response and determines the next step in the process. If an operation fails, the orchestrator initiates compensating actions to revert previous operations.
- **Advantages**:
- **Centralized Control**: The orchestrator provides a single point of control, making it easier to manage the saga's flow and logic.
- **Simplified Error Handling**: Error handling is centralized, allowing for consistent compensating actions and recovery processes.
- **Disadvantages**:
- **Single Point of Failure**: If the orchestrator fails, it can disrupt the entire saga.
- **Reduced Scalability**: The orchestrator can become a bottleneck if it must handle a large number of requests simultaneously.

2. Choreography

In a choreographed saga, each service involved in the saga is responsible for publishing and reacting to events. There is no central coordinator; instead, each service listens for events and acts based on those events.

- **How It Works**: When a service completes its operation, it publishes an event to an event bus or message broker. Other services listen for these events and respond accordingly. If a service encounters an error, it can publish a compensating event to notify other services to perform rollback actions.
- **Advantages**:
- **Decentralization**: Choreography removes the single point of failure and allows for greater resilience in the system.
- **Improved Scalability**: Each service operates independently, allowing for better scalability and resource utilization.
- **Disadvantages**:
- **Complex Coordination**: Managing the overall flow of the saga can be

more complex due to the lack of centralized control.

- **Difficult Error Handling**: Compensating actions must be handled by each service, making it more challenging to ensure consistency.

Implementing the Saga Pattern

Implementing the saga pattern in a microservices architecture requires careful consideration of how to manage the flow of operations and compensating transactions. Below are steps and best practices for implementing the saga pattern effectively.

1. Identify the Workflow

The first step in implementing a saga is to identify the workflow that needs to be managed. This involves determining the sequence of operations required to complete the transaction and identifying the services involved. For example, in an online shopping application, the workflow for placing an order may include the following steps:

- Create an order in the order service.
- Reserve inventory in the inventory service.
- Process payment in the payment service.
- Notify the user through the notification service.

2. Choose an Execution Model

Once the workflow is defined, decide whether to use orchestration or choreography for managing the saga. This choice will depend on factors such as the complexity of the workflow, the need for centralized control, and the resilience requirements of the application.

3. Define Compensating Transactions

For each operation in the saga, define the compensating transaction that will be executed in case of failure. Compensating transactions should be carefully designed to reverse the effects of the original operation. For example, if the payment service fails after the inventory has been reserved, the compensating transaction for the inventory service would release the reserved inventory.

4. Implement Event Communication

Set up the necessary infrastructure for event communication between services. This may involve using message brokers (e.g., RabbitMQ, Kafka) or event buses (e.g., AWS SNS) to facilitate the publishing and consumption of events.

- **Publish Events**: Services should publish events when they complete their operations. For example, the order service could publish an event like "OrderCreated" after successfully creating an order.
- **Listen for Events**: Services should subscribe to relevant events and respond accordingly. For instance, the inventory service should listen for the "OrderCreated" event to reserve inventory.

5. Error Handling and Compensation

Implement error handling mechanisms within each service to detect failures and initiate compensating transactions when necessary. For example, if the payment service encounters an error, it should publish a compensating event to inform other services to revert their actions.

- **Retry Logic**: Consider implementing retry logic for transient errors, allowing operations to be retried before initiating compensating transactions.
- **Timeouts**: Set timeouts for operations to avoid blocking the saga indefinitely.

6. Monitor and Log Saga Execution

Implement monitoring and logging to track the execution of the saga and detect any failures. Use distributed tracing tools to visualize the flow of events and identify bottlenecks or issues in the workflow.

Real-World Use Cases of the Saga Pattern

The saga pattern is widely applicable across various domains and use cases. Below are some common scenarios where the saga pattern can effectively manage distributed transactions.

1. E-Commerce Applications

In an e-commerce application, placing an order typically involves multiple services: order management, inventory management, payment processing, and notification. The saga pattern can be used to manage the workflow for placing an order, ensuring that each service performs its tasks correctly and that any failures are handled gracefully.

Example Workflow:

- **Order Service**: Creates an order and publishes an "OrderCreated" event.
- **Inventory Service**: Listens for the event, reserves the necessary inventory, and publishes an "InventoryReserved" event.
- **Payment Service**: Listens for the event, processes the payment, and publishes a "PaymentProcessed" event.
- **Notification Service**: Listens for the event and sends a confirmation email to the customer.

If any step fails, compensating transactions are triggered to revert the actions taken by previous services.

2. Travel Booking Systems

In travel booking applications, creating a trip often involves multiple services, such as flight booking, hotel reservations, and car rentals. The saga pattern can be employed to manage the booking process, ensuring that each service completes its task while maintaining data consistency.

Example Workflow:

- **Flight Booking Service**: Books a flight and publishes a "FlightBooked" event.
- **Hotel Reservation Service**: Listens for the event, reserves a hotel room,

60

and publishes a "HotelReserved" event.

- **Car Rental Service**: Listens for the event, reserves a car, and publishes a "CarReserved" event.

If the flight booking fails after the hotel is reserved, the saga pattern ensures that compensating actions are taken to cancel the hotel reservation.

3. Financial Transactions

In financial applications, managing transactions across multiple services is critical for maintaining data integrity. The saga pattern can be used to coordinate operations such as fund transfers, account updates, and transaction logging.

Example Workflow:

- **Transfer Service**: Initiates a fund transfer and publishes a "TransferInitiated" event.
- **Debit Service**: Listens for the event, debits the sender's account, and publishes a "FundsDebited" event.
- **Credit Service**: Listens for the event, credits the receiver's account, and publishes a "FundsCredited" event.

If any step fails, compensating transactions are triggered to revert the changes made by previous services.

Best Practices for Implementing the Saga Pattern

To ensure successful implementation of the saga pattern in microservices architectures, consider the following best practices:

1. **Clearly Define Workflows**: Clearly define the workflows and identify the operations that need to be performed for each saga. This clarity helps in designing compensating transactions and ensures that all necessary steps are accounted for.
2. **Implement Robust Error Handling**: Design robust error handling

mechanisms for each service involved in the saga. Ensure that services can detect failures and initiate compensating transactions when necessary.

3. **Choose the Right Execution Model**: Decide between orchestration and choreography based on the complexity of the workflow and the need for centralized control. Choose the model that best fits the requirements of your application.

4. **Use Event-Driven Communication**: Leverage event-driven communication to decouple services and facilitate asynchronous processing. This allows for better scalability and responsiveness in the overall system.

5. **Monitor and Trace**: Implement monitoring and tracing to gain visibility into the execution of sagas. Use distributed tracing tools to track the flow of events and identify any bottlenecks or issues.

6. **Test Compensating Transactions**: Thoroughly test compensating transactions to ensure they correctly revert changes made by previous operations. This testing is crucial for maintaining data consistency and integrity.

7. **Documentation**: Document the saga workflows, including the sequence of operations, compensating transactions, and any dependencies between services. Clear documentation helps developers understand the design and ensures smooth maintenance.

Conclusion

The Saga Pattern is a powerful solution for managing distributed transactions in microservices architectures. By breaking down transactions into smaller, independent operations and utilizing compensating transactions, the saga pattern ensures data consistency while allowing for flexibility and scalability.

This chapter explored the key characteristics of the saga pattern, the two execution models (orchestration and choreography), and the steps for implementing sagas in your applications. We also discussed real-world use cases where the saga pattern can effectively manage complex workflows, and we provided best practices for ensuring successful implementation.

As we continue our exploration of microservices design patterns, we will delve into additional strategies and techniques for building resilient and efficient serverless applications, equipping you with the knowledge to navigate the complexities of modern software development.

Chapter 6: Resiliency Patterns in Serverless Applications

I n modern software architectures, particularly in the realm of microservices and serverless computing, the concept of resiliency has emerged as a critical concern. Resiliency is the ability of an application to gracefully handle failures and recover from them, ensuring minimal disruption to the user experience and business operations. Given the distributed nature of serverless applications, where multiple services communicate over networks, achieving resiliency requires a thoughtful approach to design and implementation.

This chapter delves into various resiliency patterns applicable to serverless applications, exploring their principles, implementation strategies, and best practices. By understanding and applying these patterns, developers can build robust and resilient serverless applications capable of withstanding failures and maintaining availability.

Understanding Resiliency in Serverless Applications

Resiliency is a multifaceted concept that encompasses various aspects of application design and operation. In the context of serverless computing, resiliency involves addressing challenges related to network latency, transient failures, resource limitations, and service availability. The goal is to ensure that serverless applications remain operational even in the face of unexpected failures.

Key Aspects of Resiliency

1. **Fault Tolerance**: The ability of an application to continue functioning correctly in the presence of failures. This may involve automatically retrying failed operations, invoking fallback mechanisms, or gracefully degrading functionality.

2. **Graceful Degradation**: When a system cannot fulfill a request as intended, it should degrade gracefully, providing a partial response or alternative functionality rather than failing completely. For example, if a recommendation service is unavailable, an e-commerce application might display a generic message instead of failing to load product suggestions.

3. **Redundancy**: Implementing redundant components or services to ensure that if one instance fails, another can take over. This redundancy can be achieved through multiple instances of serverless functions or services, often deployed across different regions or availability zones.

4. **Circuit Breaker**: A design pattern that prevents a system from trying to execute an operation that is likely to fail. If a service is experiencing issues, the circuit breaker "opens," and subsequent requests are immediately failed, allowing the service time to recover.

5. **Retry Logic**: Automatically retrying failed requests or operations can be an effective way to handle transient failures. Implementing exponential backoff for retries can help avoid overwhelming a service that is temporarily unavailable.

6. **Monitoring and Alerting**: Continuous monitoring of application performance and health is essential for identifying issues before they escalate. Implementing robust logging, metrics collection, and alerting mechanisms helps teams respond to failures promptly.

Resiliency Patterns for Serverless Applications

There are several established patterns that can enhance the resiliency of serverless applications. This section will explore key resiliency patterns, including the Retry Pattern, Circuit Breaker Pattern, Timeout Pattern, Bulkhead Pattern, and Fallback Pattern.

1. Retry Pattern

The **Retry Pattern** is a straightforward yet effective way to enhance the resiliency of serverless applications. When a request fails due to transient errors (such as network timeouts or brief service outages), automatically retrying the request can lead to successful execution.

How It Works:

- When a service call fails, the application waits for a predetermined interval and then attempts the request again. This process can be repeated a specified number of times before giving up.
- To prevent overwhelming a service that is struggling, the retries should be spaced out using a technique known as **exponential backoff**, which gradually increases the wait time between retries.

Example: Consider a serverless function that retrieves user data from a remote API. If the initial request fails due to a network timeout, the function can automatically retry the request a few times before returning an error response to the client.

Considerations:

- **Idempotency**: Ensure that the operation being retried is idempotent, meaning that repeated executions of the same request do not lead to unintended side effects. For instance, retrying a request to create a new order might result in duplicate orders unless the operation is designed to handle such cases.
- **Limit the Number of Retries**: Set a maximum number of retries to avoid indefinite waiting for a successful response. If the service remains

unavailable after the retries, the application should gracefully handle the failure.

2. Circuit Breaker Pattern

The **Circuit Breaker Pattern** is a critical resiliency pattern that helps prevent a service from becoming overwhelmed when it is experiencing problems. It acts as a protective mechanism that temporarily blocks requests to a failing service, allowing the service time to recover.

How It Works:

- The circuit breaker has three states: **Closed, Open**, and **Half-Open**.
- **Closed**: The circuit breaker allows requests to pass through to the service. If the service responds successfully, the circuit remains closed.
- **Open**: When the failure threshold is exceeded (e.g., consecutive failed requests), the circuit breaker opens, blocking all requests to the service. During this time, the application can return fallback responses to clients.
- **Half-Open**: After a predetermined timeout period, the circuit breaker enters the half-open state, allowing a limited number of requests to pass through. If these requests succeed, the circuit returns to the closed state; if they fail, it remains open.

Example: In an e-commerce application, if the payment service experiences repeated failures, the circuit breaker can open to prevent the order service from overwhelming it with requests. Instead of failing all orders, the order service can return a message indicating that the payment service is temporarily unavailable.

Considerations:

- **Failure Threshold**: Define an appropriate threshold for determining when to open the circuit. This could be based on the number of consecutive failures or a failure rate over a specified time window.
- **Timeouts**: Configure timeout periods for the open state and the half-open state to balance responsiveness and recovery.

3. Timeout Pattern

The **Timeout Pattern** involves setting a maximum duration for operations or requests to complete. If an operation exceeds this duration, it is automatically aborted, and an appropriate response is returned to the client.

How It Works:

- When a service call is made, a timeout is set for the expected duration of the operation. If the operation does not complete within this timeframe, it is considered a failure, and the application can take appropriate actions (e.g., logging the error, returning a fallback response).

Example: In a serverless function that calls an external API to retrieve user data, a timeout can be set to ensure that if the API does not respond within a specified period (e.g., 2 seconds), the function will abort the request and return an error message.

Considerations:

- **Appropriate Timeout Values**: Set timeout values based on the expected response times of external services. Too short a timeout may lead to unnecessary failures, while too long a timeout can delay error handling.
- **Graceful Degradation**: Implement fallback mechanisms to ensure that users receive informative responses even when a timeout occurs.

4. Bulkhead Pattern

The **Bulkhead Pattern** is a resiliency pattern that isolates different parts of a system to prevent failures from cascading across components. By dividing resources into isolated groups (or bulkheads), the impact of failures can be contained, ensuring that the overall system remains operational.

How It Works:

- The bulkhead pattern involves segmenting resources, such as thread pools, service instances, or database connections, so that failures in one area do not affect others. This isolation allows the application to continue functioning even when some parts experience issues.

Example: In a serverless application that integrates with multiple third-party services, the application can allocate separate thread pools for each service. If one service experiences a high volume of requests and fails, the other services can continue to operate without being affected.

Considerations:

- **Resource Allocation**: Determine how to allocate resources across bulkheads based on expected workloads and usage patterns.
- **Monitoring**: Implement monitoring to track the performance and health of each bulkhead, ensuring that isolated failures can be identified and addressed promptly.

5. Fallback Pattern

The **Fallback Pattern** is used to define alternative responses or actions that can be taken when a service fails or encounters an issue. By providing fallback options, the application can maintain functionality and improve the user experience even in the face of failures.

How It Works:

- When a service call fails, the application can fall back to a predefined alternative response or behavior. This can include returning cached data, providing default values, or executing alternative logic.

Example: In a news aggregator application, if a service that fetches the latest articles from an external API fails, the application can fall back to displaying cached articles from the previous day. This ensures that users still receive relevant content even when the external service is unavailable.

Considerations:

- **Fallback Strategies**: Define appropriate fallback strategies based on the use case. Consider the impact on user experience and data integrity when choosing fallback options.

- **Monitoring and Alerts**: Monitor the frequency of fallback executions to identify underlying issues with dependent services.

Implementing Resiliency Patterns in Serverless Applications

To effectively implement resiliency patterns in serverless applications, developers should follow a structured approach that considers design, implementation, and monitoring. Below are steps and best practices for implementing resiliency patterns in serverless applications.

1. Design for Resiliency

Begin by designing your serverless architecture with resiliency in mind. Identify potential points of failure, understand dependencies between services, and define how each service will respond to failures.

- **Identify Critical Services**: Determine which services are critical to the operation of the application and assess their failure impact.
- **Define Failure Scenarios**: Analyze potential failure scenarios for each service, including transient errors, network issues, and service outages.

2. Choose the Right Patterns

Select the resiliency patterns that best fit your application's needs. Depending on the complexity of the system, a combination of patterns may be appropriate.

- **Combine Patterns**: Consider using multiple resiliency patterns together. For instance, combining the Circuit Breaker and Retry patterns can enhance the overall robustness of the system.

3. Implement Resiliency Logic

Implement the chosen resiliency patterns within your serverless functions. This includes adding retry logic, circuit breakers, timeouts, and fallback mechanisms.

- **Use Libraries**: Leverage libraries and frameworks that provide built-in support for resiliency patterns. For example, libraries like Polly (for .NET) and Resilience4j (for Java) can simplify the implementation of these patterns.

4. Monitor and Log

Implement monitoring and logging to track the health of your serverless applications. Use cloud provider tools (e.g., AWS CloudWatch, Azure Monitor) to collect metrics, logs, and traces.

- **Set Up Alerts**: Configure alerts for key performance indicators (KPIs) such as error rates, latency, and the frequency of fallback executions. This allows for proactive responses to issues.

5. Test Resiliency

Conduct thorough testing to validate the resiliency of your serverless applications. Simulate failures and observe how the application responds to ensure that fallback mechanisms and compensating actions work as intended.

- **Chaos Engineering**: Consider using chaos engineering principles to intentionally introduce failures into your system and observe its behavior. This helps identify weaknesses and areas for improvement.

Real-World Use Cases of Resiliency Patterns

Resiliency patterns are applicable across various domains and use cases. Below are some common scenarios where these patterns can effectively enhance the robustness of serverless applications.

1. E-Commerce Applications

In e-commerce applications, maintaining availability and performance is critical for user satisfaction. Implementing resiliency patterns can help manage distributed transactions and ensure smooth operations even during peak traffic.

Example: An e-commerce application can utilize the Circuit Breaker pattern to protect the payment service from overload during high-demand periods. If the payment service begins to fail, the circuit breaker opens, allowing the application to provide a fallback response to users while preventing further strain on the service.

2. Financial Services

In financial applications, data integrity and availability are paramount. Implementing resiliency patterns can help ensure that transactions are processed reliably and that users receive timely responses.

Example: A bank's fund transfer service can employ the Retry and Fallback patterns. If a transfer request fails due to a temporary network issue, the application can automatically retry the operation. If the retries fail, the application can provide a fallback response to inform the user of the issue while logging the error for further investigation.

3. IoT Applications

In Internet of Things (IoT) applications, devices often communicate with cloud services to send data and receive commands. Resiliency patterns can help ensure that communication remains reliable even in the face of network disruptions.

Example: An IoT application can utilize the Bulkhead pattern to isolate communication channels for different devices. If one device experiences connectivity issues, it does not affect the communication of other devices, ensuring that the application remains operational.

Best Practices for Implementing Resiliency Patterns

To ensure successful implementation of resiliency patterns in serverless applications, consider the following best practices:

1. **Start Simple**: Begin with a small set of resiliency patterns and gradually expand as needed. Avoid over-engineering the application from the outset.
2. **Document Patterns**: Clearly document the resiliency patterns imple-

mented in your application. This helps ensure that all team members understand the design and can maintain it effectively.

3. **Continuously Monitor**: Implement continuous monitoring to track the performance of resiliency patterns. Regularly review metrics and logs to identify areas for improvement.

4. **Adapt to Changes**: Be prepared to adapt resiliency patterns as the application evolves. New features, services, or changing traffic patterns may necessitate adjustments to the existing design.

5. **Educate Teams**: Ensure that development teams are educated on resiliency patterns and their importance. Foster a culture of resilience within the organization to promote best practices across teams.

Conclusion

Resiliency is a fundamental aspect of building robust serverless applications. By implementing resiliency patterns such as Retry, Circuit Breaker, Timeout, Bulkhead, and Fallback, developers can effectively manage failures and ensure that applications remain operational under varying conditions.

This chapter explored the key concepts of resiliency in serverless applications, the various resiliency patterns, and strategies for implementation. We also discussed real-world use cases and best practices for ensuring successful implementation.

As we continue our exploration of microservices design patterns, we will delve into additional strategies and techniques for building resilient and efficient serverless applications, equipping you with the knowledge to navigate the complexities of modern software development.

Chapter 7: Security Best Practices for Serverless Applications

A s organizations increasingly adopt serverless computing, security has emerged as a critical concern. While serverless architectures offer numerous benefits, such as reduced operational overhead and automatic scaling, they also introduce unique security challenges that must be addressed. This chapter will explore security best practices for serverless applications, covering key considerations, common vulnerabilities, and strategies for mitigating risks. By implementing these best practices, organizations can enhance the security posture of their serverless applications and protect sensitive data.

Understanding Security in Serverless Architectures

Serverless architectures inherently change the way applications are built, deployed, and managed. In a traditional environment, organizations have direct control over servers, operating systems, and middleware. However, in a serverless environment, much of this control is delegated to cloud service providers, which creates a shared responsibility model for security.

Key Security Considerations

1. **Shared Responsibility Model**: In a serverless architecture, the cloud

provider is responsible for securing the underlying infrastructure, while the customer is responsible for securing their applications and data. Understanding this model is essential for identifying security responsibilities.

2. **Decentralized Architecture**: Serverless applications often comprise multiple microservices that communicate over APIs. This decentralization increases the attack surface, requiring comprehensive security measures across all components.

3. **Dynamic Nature**: Serverless functions are ephemeral and stateless, which makes it challenging to apply traditional security controls. The dynamic nature of serverless computing demands that security measures be adaptable and capable of addressing rapid changes in the application environment.

4. **Event-Driven Architecture**: Many serverless applications rely on event-driven architectures, where services react to events from various sources. This can introduce security risks, particularly if events are not properly validated or authenticated.

Common Vulnerabilities in Serverless Applications

To effectively secure serverless applications, it's important to understand the common vulnerabilities that can arise. Some of the most prevalent vulnerabilities include:

1. **Insecure APIs**: Since serverless applications often expose APIs for communication, poorly secured APIs can lead to unauthorized access, data breaches, and injection attacks.

2. **Excessive Permissions**: Serverless functions typically require permissions to access other resources (e.g., databases, storage, external APIs). Granting excessive permissions increases the risk of data exposure and potential misuse.

3. **Lack of Input Validation**: Input validation is crucial for preventing injection attacks, such as SQL injection or cross-site scripting (XSS).

Failing to validate incoming data can lead to security vulnerabilities.

4. **Insecure Dependencies**: Serverless functions often rely on third-party libraries and packages. Vulnerabilities in these dependencies can introduce risks to the application.

5. **Data Exposure**: Sensitive data can be inadvertently exposed if not properly encrypted or if access controls are not enforced. This can lead to compliance violations and data breaches.

6. **Poor Logging and Monitoring**: Inadequate logging and monitoring can hinder the ability to detect and respond to security incidents. Without visibility into application behavior, organizations may struggle to identify breaches or anomalies.

Security Best Practices for Serverless Applications

Implementing security best practices is essential for protecting serverless applications from potential vulnerabilities. This section outlines key practices that organizations should adopt to enhance the security of their serverless environments.

1. Secure APIs

- **Authentication and Authorization**: Implement strong authentication mechanisms to ensure that only authorized users can access your APIs. Consider using industry-standard protocols like OAuth2 or OpenID Connect for secure access.
- **Input Validation**: Validate all incoming requests to ensure that they conform to expected formats and do not contain malicious content. Use whitelisting approaches to restrict allowed input values.
- **Rate Limiting**: Implement rate limiting on APIs to prevent abuse and mitigate the risk of denial-of-service attacks. Define thresholds for the number of requests a client can make within a specific time period.
- **Use HTTPS**: Always use HTTPS for API communication to encrypt data in transit. This protects against eavesdropping and man-in-the-middle attacks.

- **API Gateway**: Utilize an API gateway to manage API traffic, enforce security policies, and provide a centralized point for logging and monitoring API requests.

2. Principle of Least Privilege

- **Granular Permissions**: Follow the principle of least privilege by granting only the minimum permissions necessary for each serverless function to perform its tasks. Avoid granting broad permissions that can expose sensitive resources.
- **Use IAM Roles**: Implement Identity and Access Management (IAM) roles to control access to AWS services. Define roles for each function and specify the permissions needed to interact with other resources.
- **Regularly Review Permissions**: Periodically review and audit permissions to ensure that they remain aligned with the current application requirements. Revoke any unnecessary permissions promptly.

3. Secure Data Storage

- **Encryption**: Encrypt sensitive data both at rest and in transit. Use encryption services provided by your cloud provider (e.g., AWS KMS, Azure Key Vault) to manage encryption keys securely.
- **Access Control**: Implement strict access control policies for data storage solutions (e.g., databases, object storage). Ensure that only authorized serverless functions can access sensitive data.
- **Data Masking**: Use data masking techniques to protect sensitive information when it is accessed or displayed. This can help prevent data exposure during development or testing.

4. Secure Dependencies

- **Use Trusted Libraries**: Only use third-party libraries and packages from trusted sources. Review the security of dependencies before integrating them into your serverless functions.

- **Dependency Scanning**: Implement automated tools to scan dependencies for known vulnerabilities. Tools like Snyk and OWASP Dependency-Check can help identify security issues in libraries.
- **Regular Updates**: Keep dependencies up to date by regularly applying security patches and updates. Schedule periodic reviews to ensure that all libraries are current.

5. Logging and Monitoring

- **Centralized Logging**: Implement centralized logging for all serverless functions. Use cloud provider services (e.g., AWS CloudWatch Logs, Azure Monitor) to collect and store logs for analysis.
- **Event Monitoring**: Set up monitoring for key events, such as API calls, function executions, and error occurrences. This enables timely detection of anomalies and security incidents.
- **Alerting**: Configure alerts for critical events or thresholds, such as unusual error rates or unauthorized access attempts. Prompt alerts can help teams respond quickly to potential security breaches.

6. Continuous Security Testing

- **Automated Security Testing**: Integrate security testing into the development lifecycle. Use automated tools to conduct static analysis, dynamic analysis, and penetration testing on serverless functions.
- **Threat Modeling**: Conduct threat modeling exercises to identify potential vulnerabilities and attack vectors. Regularly update threat models to reflect changes in the application or environment.
- **Regular Security Audits**: Perform regular security audits and assessments to evaluate the overall security posture of your serverless applications. This can help identify areas for improvement and ensure compliance with industry standards.

7. Incident Response Plan

- **Define Incident Response Procedures**: Develop and document incident response procedures to address potential security breaches. Ensure that all team members understand their roles and responsibilities in the event of an incident.
- **Conduct Drills and Simulations**: Regularly conduct incident response drills and simulations to test the effectiveness of your response plan. This helps ensure that the team is prepared to respond effectively to real incidents.
- **Post-Incident Reviews**: After any security incident, conduct a thorough review to analyze the response and identify lessons learned. Use this information to improve security practices and refine the incident response plan.

Compliance Considerations

In addition to implementing security best practices, organizations must also consider compliance with relevant regulations and standards. Many industries have specific requirements for data protection, privacy, and security.

Key Compliance Frameworks

1. **GDPR (General Data Protection Regulation)**: The GDPR sets strict guidelines for the collection and processing of personal data within the European Union. Organizations must implement measures to protect personal data and ensure that individuals have rights regarding their data.
2. **HIPAA (Health Insurance Portability and Accountability Act)**: HIPAA establishes standards for the protection of sensitive patient health information in the healthcare sector. Organizations must implement safeguards to secure electronic protected health information (ePHI).
3. **PCI DSS (Payment Card Industry Data Security Standard)**: PCI DSS

is a set of security standards designed to protect cardholder data during payment transactions. Organizations that handle payment information must comply with these standards to ensure secure processing.

4. **ISO 27001**: ISO 27001 is an international standard for information security management systems (ISMS). Achieving certification demonstrates an organization's commitment to managing and protecting sensitive information.

Real-World Use Cases of Security Best Practices

Implementing security best practices in serverless applications can significantly enhance their security posture. Below are some real-world scenarios where these practices can be applied effectively.

1. E-Commerce Applications

In an e-commerce application, security is paramount due to the handling of sensitive customer data and payment information. Implementing robust security measures can help protect against data breaches and fraud.

Example:

- **API Security**: Implement strong authentication mechanisms (e.g., OAuth2) to secure payment and user data APIs. Regularly review access controls and ensure that sensitive operations are only accessible to authorized users.
- **Data Encryption**: Use encryption to protect sensitive customer information, such as credit card details and personal data, during transmission and storage.

2. Financial Services

In financial services applications, safeguarding customer data and transaction integrity is critical. Applying security best practices can mitigate the risks associated with handling sensitive financial information.

Example:

- **Continuous Monitoring**: Implement continuous monitoring and alerting for suspicious activities, such as unusual transaction patterns or unauthorized access attempts.
- **Incident Response Plan**: Develop a comprehensive incident response plan to address potential security breaches quickly and effectively. Conduct regular drills to ensure that the team is prepared to respond to incidents.

3. Healthcare Applications

In healthcare applications, protecting patient data and complying with regulations such as HIPAA is essential. Implementing security best practices helps ensure the confidentiality and integrity of sensitive health information.
Example:

- **Access Control**: Implement role-based access control (RBAC) to restrict access to patient health records based on user roles. Ensure that only authorized personnel can access sensitive information.
- **Data Masking**: Use data masking techniques to protect sensitive patient information during development and testing. This helps prevent unauthorized access to real patient data.

Conclusion

Security is a paramount consideration for serverless applications, and implementing best practices is essential for safeguarding sensitive data and maintaining compliance with regulations. By understanding the unique security challenges posed by serverless architectures and adopting strategies such as secure APIs, the principle of least privilege, data encryption, and continuous monitoring, organizations can significantly enhance the security of their applications.

This chapter explored key security best practices for serverless applications, common vulnerabilities, and real-world use cases where these practices can be applied effectively. As we continue to navigate the complexities of serverless computing, a proactive approach to security will be essential for building resilient, secure, and compliant applications in today's digital landscape.

In the following chapters, we will explore additional strategies and techniques for optimizing serverless applications, providing further insights into building robust systems that leverage the power of modern cloud computing.

Chapter 8: Monitoring and Observability in Serverless Applications

I
n the world of serverless computing, applications are often built using microservices that interact with various resources and external services. While serverless architectures offer scalability and reduced operational overhead, they also introduce complexities in monitoring and observability. Ensuring the performance, reliability, and security of serverless applications requires robust monitoring and observability practices. This chapter will explore the importance of monitoring and observability in serverless environments, various tools and techniques, and best practices for implementing effective monitoring solutions.

Understanding Monitoring and Observability

Definitions

1. **Monitoring**: Monitoring involves the continuous collection and analysis of metrics, logs, and events to assess the performance and health of an application. In serverless architectures, monitoring helps identify issues, track usage patterns, and optimize resource utilization.

2. **Observability**: Observability goes beyond monitoring by providing insights into the internal state of an application based on external

outputs. It encompasses the ability to understand how the application behaves under different conditions and to diagnose issues effectively. Observability relies on a combination of metrics, logs, and traces to provide a comprehensive view of the application's performance.

Importance of Monitoring and Observability

Monitoring and observability are critical for several reasons:

1. **Performance Optimization**: Continuous monitoring allows organizations to identify performance bottlenecks and optimize resource utilization. By analyzing metrics such as latency, throughput, and error rates, teams can make informed decisions to improve application performance.
2. **Issue Detection**: Early detection of issues is crucial for maintaining application reliability. Monitoring enables teams to identify anomalies and failures before they impact users, allowing for quick remediation.
3. **Debugging and Troubleshooting**: When issues arise, observability provides the insights needed to diagnose problems effectively. By analyzing logs and traces, teams can pinpoint the root cause of failures and implement fixes.
4. **Cost Management**: Monitoring resource usage can help organizations manage costs in serverless environments. By understanding usage patterns, teams can optimize function execution and reduce unnecessary expenses.
5. **User Experience**: Monitoring ensures that applications perform reliably, leading to a better user experience. By maintaining high availability and performance, organizations can meet user expectations and build trust.

Key Metrics to Monitor in Serverless Applications

To effectively monitor serverless applications, teams should focus on specific key metrics that provide insights into performance and health. The following are essential metrics to track:

1. Function Execution Metrics

- **Invocation Count**: The number of times a function is invoked. This metric helps track usage patterns and can inform scaling decisions.
- **Execution Duration**: The time taken to execute a function. Monitoring execution duration can help identify performance issues and optimize code efficiency.
- **Error Rate**: The percentage of failed invocations compared to the total number of invocations. A high error rate may indicate underlying issues that require attention.
- **Concurrency**: The number of concurrent executions of a function. Monitoring concurrency helps ensure that the application can handle spikes in traffic and manage resource limits effectively.

2. API Gateway Metrics

- **Request Count**: The total number of requests received by the API Gateway. This metric helps track traffic patterns and user engagement.
- **Response Time**: The time taken to respond to requests. Monitoring response time can help identify latency issues and improve user experience.
- **4xx and 5xx Error Rates**: The rates of client errors (4xx) and server errors (5xx). High error rates can indicate problems with API endpoints or backend services.

3. Resource Utilization Metrics

- **Memory Usage**: The amount of memory consumed by serverless functions. Monitoring memory usage helps identify potential resource constraints and optimize function performance.
- **Timeouts**: The number of functions that exceed their timeout limits. Tracking timeouts can indicate performance issues or inefficient code.
- **Cold Start Latency**: The additional latency experienced when a function is invoked after being idle. Monitoring cold starts is essential for understanding the impact on user experience.

4. Business Metrics

- **Transaction Volume**: The number of transactions processed by the application. Tracking transaction volume helps assess business performance and user engagement.
- **Conversion Rates**: The percentage of users who complete desired actions, such as making a purchase. Monitoring conversion rates can provide insights into application effectiveness.
- **User Retention**: The percentage of users who return to the application after their initial visit. Monitoring user retention helps assess user satisfaction and application value.

Tools for Monitoring and Observability

A variety of tools are available for monitoring and observability in serverless applications. These tools can help collect metrics, logs, and traces, providing valuable insights into application performance and health. Below are some popular tools for monitoring and observability in serverless environments.

1. AWS CloudWatch

AWS CloudWatch is a monitoring and observability service provided by Amazon Web Services (AWS). It offers a range of features for collecting and tracking metrics, logs, and events from AWS resources, including serverless functions (AWS Lambda).

- **Key Features**:
- Custom Metrics: Users can define and publish custom metrics for monitoring specific application behavior.
- Alarms: CloudWatch allows users to set up alarms based on specified thresholds for metrics, enabling proactive notifications for issues.
- Log Management: CloudWatch Logs provides centralized log management for AWS Lambda functions, enabling teams to search, filter, and analyze logs.

2. Azure Monitor

Azure Monitor is a comprehensive monitoring solution offered by Microsoft Azure. It provides visibility into application performance and resource utilization across Azure services, including serverless functions (Azure Functions).

- **Key Features**:
- Application Insights: A powerful component of Azure Monitor that offers deep insights into application performance, user behavior, and exceptions.
- Custom Dashboards: Users can create custom dashboards to visualize key metrics and monitor application health in real-time.
- Alerts and Notifications: Azure Monitor allows users to configure alerts based on performance metrics and resource utilization.

3. Google Cloud Operations Suite (formerly Stackdriver)

The **Google Cloud Operations Suite** is a monitoring and observability solution for applications running on Google Cloud Platform (GCP). It provides integrated monitoring, logging, and diagnostics for serverless applications (Google Cloud Functions).

- **Key Features**:
- Logging: Centralized logging capabilities for capturing logs from Google Cloud Functions and other GCP services.
- Monitoring Dashboards: Users can create customizable dashboards to visualize key metrics and gain insights into application performance.
- Error Reporting: Automatic error reporting helps identify and track application errors, making it easier to troubleshoot issues.

4. OpenTelemetry

OpenTelemetry is an open-source observability framework that provides APIs, libraries, and instrumentation for collecting metrics, logs, and traces. It is designed to work with various cloud platforms and services, making it a flexible option for monitoring serverless applications.

- **Key Features**:
- Language Support: OpenTelemetry supports multiple programming languages, allowing developers to instrument applications in their preferred language.
- Vendor Agnostic: As an open-source solution, OpenTelemetry can integrate with various observability backends, including AWS CloudWatch, Azure Monitor, and Google Cloud Operations Suite.
- Distributed Tracing: OpenTelemetry provides distributed tracing capabilities, enabling teams to visualize the flow of requests across services.

5. Third-Party Monitoring Solutions

In addition to cloud-native monitoring tools, there are several third-party solutions that provide enhanced monitoring and observability capabilities for serverless applications. Some popular options include:

- **Datadog**: A cloud monitoring and analytics platform that offers powerful monitoring, logging, and APM (Application Performance Monitoring) capabilities for serverless applications.
- **New Relic**: An observability platform that provides insights into application performance, user experience, and infrastructure health.
- **Dynatrace**: An AI-powered monitoring solution that offers automatic discovery, monitoring, and performance optimization for serverless applications.

Implementing Monitoring and Observability Practices

To effectively implement monitoring and observability practices in serverless applications, organizations should follow a structured approach. This section outlines key steps and best practices for establishing robust monitoring and observability solutions.

1. Define Monitoring Goals and Objectives

Before implementing monitoring solutions, organizations should define their monitoring goals and objectives. This involves identifying the key metrics, logs, and traces that will provide valuable insights into application performance and health.

- **Identify Critical Metrics**: Determine which metrics are essential for tracking application performance, user experience, and business outcomes.
- **Define Success Criteria**: Establish success criteria for monitoring,

89

including acceptable performance thresholds, error rates, and response times.

2. Instrument Applications for Monitoring

Proper instrumentation of serverless functions and associated services is crucial for collecting relevant metrics, logs, and traces. This may involve using built-in monitoring features provided by cloud platforms or integrating third-party libraries.

- **Use Monitoring Libraries**: Leverage libraries and SDKs that facilitate instrumentation for monitoring solutions. For example, AWS X-Ray SDKs can be used to instrument AWS Lambda functions for distributed tracing.
- **Enable Logging**: Ensure that logging is enabled for serverless functions to capture relevant application events and errors.

3. Set Up Monitoring Tools

Select and configure the appropriate monitoring tools based on your application's requirements and cloud provider. This may involve setting up dashboards, alerts, and reporting mechanisms.

- **Create Dashboards**: Design customizable dashboards that visualize key metrics and provide insights into application performance. Dashboards should be tailored to the needs of different stakeholders (e.g., developers, operations teams).
- **Configure Alerts**: Set up alerts for critical events, such as high error rates, increased latency, or resource utilization thresholds. Alerts should be actionable and provide context for troubleshooting.

4. Implement Distributed Tracing

Distributed tracing is essential for understanding the flow of requests across serverless functions and services. Implementing distributed tracing allows teams to visualize the interactions between components and identify performance bottlenecks.

- **Use OpenTelemetry**: Implement OpenTelemetry to instrument serverless functions for distributed tracing. This enables tracking of requests as they traverse multiple services.
- **Analyze Trace Data**: Regularly analyze trace data to identify latency issues, service dependencies, and performance bottlenecks.

5. Monitor Logs

Effective log management is critical for troubleshooting and diagnosing issues in serverless applications. Implement centralized logging solutions to collect and analyze logs from all serverless functions and services.

- **Centralized Log Storage**: Use cloud-native logging solutions (e.g., AWS CloudWatch Logs, Azure Monitor) to store and manage logs in a centralized location.
- **Log Analysis**: Implement tools for analyzing logs to identify patterns, anomalies, and error occurrences. Regular log analysis helps teams proactively address potential issues.

6. Continuous Improvement

Monitoring and observability should be viewed as ongoing processes that require continuous improvement. Regularly assess monitoring effectiveness and make adjustments based on evolving application needs.

- **Review Monitoring Practices**: Periodically review monitoring practices to ensure they align with business goals and technical requirements.

- **Incorporate Feedback**: Gather feedback from development and operations teams on the effectiveness of monitoring and observability solutions. Use this feedback to drive improvements.

Real-World Use Cases of Monitoring and Observability

Implementing effective monitoring and observability practices can significantly enhance the performance and reliability of serverless applications. Below are some real-world scenarios where monitoring and observability have proven beneficial.

1. E-Commerce Applications

In e-commerce applications, maintaining high availability and performance is critical for user satisfaction. Implementing monitoring and observability practices helps identify issues and optimize resource utilization.

Example:

- **Monitoring Traffic Patterns**: An e-commerce platform can use monitoring tools to track traffic patterns during peak shopping seasons. By analyzing metrics such as request counts and response times, the platform can proactively scale serverless functions to handle increased traffic.
- **Error Detection**: By monitoring error rates in the checkout process, the e-commerce platform can quickly identify issues with payment processing and take corrective actions to ensure a seamless user experience.

2. Financial Services

In financial applications, safeguarding customer data and ensuring transaction integrity are paramount. Implementing monitoring and observability practices helps organizations detect anomalies and respond to security incidents.

Example:

- **Anomaly Detection**: A financial services application can implement monitoring to detect unusual transaction patterns that may indicate fraudulent activity. By setting up alerts for abnormal transaction volumes, the organization can respond quickly to potential threats.
- **Performance Monitoring**: Monitoring the performance of payment processing services allows the financial application to identify latency issues and optimize resource allocation, ensuring timely processing of transactions.

3. IoT Applications

In IoT applications, devices communicate with cloud services to send data and receive commands. Effective monitoring and observability practices help ensure reliable communication and performance.

Example:

- **Device Monitoring**: An IoT application can implement monitoring to track the status and connectivity of devices. If a device becomes unresponsive, the application can alert administrators to investigate and resolve the issue.
- **Data Integrity Monitoring**: Monitoring data sent from IoT devices helps ensure data integrity. By analyzing data patterns and validating incoming data, the application can detect anomalies and take corrective actions.

Conclusion

Monitoring and observability are essential components of serverless applications, enabling organizations to maintain performance, reliability, and security. By implementing robust monitoring practices, teams can gain valuable insights into application behavior, identify issues proactively, and optimize resource utilization.

This chapter explored the importance of monitoring and observability in serverless architectures, key metrics to monitor, various tools available for monitoring, and best practices for effective implementation. We also discussed real-world use cases where monitoring and observability have proven beneficial.

As we continue our exploration of serverless design patterns, we will delve into additional strategies and techniques for building resilient and efficient serverless applications, equipping you with the knowledge to navigate the complexities of modern software development.

Chapter 9: Best Practices for Testing Serverless Applications

T esting is a critical aspect of software development that ensures applications function as intended, meet user requirements, and maintain a high level of quality. In serverless architectures, testing presents unique challenges and considerations due to the distributed nature of applications and the ephemeral characteristics of serverless functions. This chapter will explore best practices for testing serverless applications, covering various testing strategies, tools, and techniques that can enhance the quality and reliability of serverless systems.

Understanding Testing in Serverless Architectures

Testing serverless applications requires a different approach compared to traditional monolithic or microservices architectures. The main challenges include:

1. **Ephemeral Nature**: Serverless functions are stateless and short-lived, making it difficult to maintain context between invocations. This requires careful planning to manage state during testing.
2. **Complex Interactions**: Serverless applications often consist of multiple microservices that interact via APIs and events. Testing these

interactions requires a comprehensive understanding of the application architecture.

3. **Limited Local Environment**: The local development environment for serverless functions may not replicate the cloud environment accurately. This can lead to discrepancies between local tests and production behavior.

4. **Rapid Iteration**: Serverless applications are often developed and deployed rapidly, making it essential to implement efficient testing practices that keep pace with the development cycle.

Key Objectives of Testing

When testing serverless applications, the following objectives should be prioritized:

1. **Functional Testing**: Ensure that individual serverless functions perform their intended tasks correctly and meet specified requirements.

2. **Integration Testing**: Verify that different services and components of the application work together as expected. This includes testing interactions between serverless functions, APIs, and external services.

3. **Performance Testing**: Assess the performance and scalability of serverless applications under varying loads. This includes testing response times, throughput, and resource utilization.

4. **Security Testing**: Identify vulnerabilities and security weaknesses in serverless applications to ensure that sensitive data and resources are adequately protected.

5. **End-to-End Testing**: Validate the entire application workflow, ensuring that all components work together seamlessly to provide the desired user experience.

Testing Strategies for Serverless Applications

Several testing strategies can be employed to ensure comprehensive testing of serverless applications. These strategies encompass unit testing, integration testing, performance testing, and more. Below are the key strategies to consider:

1. Unit Testing

Unit testing involves testing individual functions or components in isolation to verify their correctness. In serverless applications, unit tests should focus on the logic within serverless functions.

Best Practices for Unit Testing

- **Use a Testing Framework**: Utilize testing frameworks appropriate for the programming language used in your serverless functions. For example, use Jest or Mocha for JavaScript, NUnit or xUnit for C#, and PyTest for Python.
- **Mock Dependencies**: Since serverless functions often interact with external services (e.g., databases, APIs), it's essential to mock these dependencies in unit tests. This allows you to isolate the function's logic and avoid dependencies on external systems during testing.
- **Test Edge Cases**: Ensure that unit tests cover various edge cases and error scenarios. This helps validate that the function behaves correctly under different conditions.
- **Automate Unit Tests**: Integrate unit tests into the continuous integration (CI) pipeline to ensure that tests are automatically executed whenever code changes are made.

2. Integration Testing

Integration testing verifies that different components of the application work together as expected. In serverless applications, integration testing is particularly important for testing interactions between serverless functions and external services.

Best Practices for Integration Testing

- **Use Staging Environments**: Set up a staging environment that closely resembles the production environment. This allows for testing in a realistic setting while minimizing the risk of affecting production data.
- **Test Real Interactions**: Unlike unit tests, integration tests should use real interactions with external services. This helps validate that the application behaves correctly when communicating with other components.
- **Manage State Carefully**: Since serverless functions are stateless, ensure that the necessary state is set up before running integration tests. Use setup and teardown methods to manage test data.
- **Automate Integration Tests**: Integrate integration tests into the CI/CD pipeline to ensure that they are executed automatically during deployments.

3. Performance Testing

Performance testing assesses how well a serverless application performs under various load conditions. This includes testing response times, throughput, and resource utilization.

Best Practices for Performance Testing

- **Simulate Load**: Use load testing tools (e.g., JMeter, Gatling, or Artillery) to simulate user traffic and assess how the application performs under load. This helps identify bottlenecks and performance issues.
- **Measure Cold Start Times**: Since serverless functions may experience

98

cold starts, it's important to measure and account for cold start times in performance tests. This helps understand the impact on user experience.

- **Monitor Resource Utilization**: Monitor resource utilization during performance tests to identify potential resource constraints. This includes tracking metrics such as memory usage, execution duration, and concurrency.
- **Conduct Stress Testing**: Perform stress testing to determine how the application behaves under extreme load conditions. This helps identify the breaking points of the application.

4. Security Testing

Security testing involves identifying vulnerabilities and weaknesses in the application to ensure that sensitive data is protected. In serverless applications, security testing is essential due to the potential exposure of APIs and the reliance on third-party services.

Best Practices for Security Testing

- **Conduct Static Analysis**: Use static analysis tools to analyze serverless function code for common vulnerabilities (e.g., SQL injection, cross-site scripting). Tools like Snyk and Bandit can help identify security issues in code.
- **Perform Dynamic Testing**: Conduct dynamic security testing (also known as penetration testing) to simulate attacks on the application and identify vulnerabilities. This helps assess the security posture of the application in a real-world context.
- **Review IAM Policies**: Regularly review IAM policies and permissions assigned to serverless functions to ensure they follow the principle of least privilege. Limit permissions to only what is necessary for the function to operate.
- **Test API Security**: Use tools to test the security of APIs exposed by serverless functions. This includes testing for authentication, authorization, and input validation.

5. End-to-End Testing

End-to-end testing validates the complete workflow of the application, ensuring that all components work together seamlessly. This type of testing is essential for verifying the user experience.

Best Practices for End-to-End Testing

- **Use Automation Tools**: Utilize automation tools (e.g., Selenium, Cypress, or TestCafe) to automate end-to-end testing. This helps ensure that tests can be run consistently and frequently.
- **Test User Scenarios**: Identify key user scenarios and workflows that should be tested end-to-end. This includes testing common user actions, such as signing up, logging in, and making purchases.
- **Monitor User Experience**: Implement monitoring tools to assess the user experience during end-to-end testing. This includes tracking response times, error rates, and user feedback.

6. Chaos Testing

Chaos testing is a proactive approach to testing that involves intentionally introducing failures into the system to observe how it behaves under adverse conditions. This helps organizations identify weaknesses and improve resilience.

Best Practices for Chaos Testing

- **Define Experiment Goals**: Clearly define the goals of chaos experiments, such as assessing the impact of network latency or simulating service failures.
- **Use Chaos Engineering Tools**: Utilize chaos engineering tools (e.g., Chaos Monkey, Gremlin, or Litmus) to orchestrate controlled failures in the system. These tools allow you to safely experiment with disruptions.
- **Monitor and Analyze**: Monitor the application during chaos experiments to assess its behavior. Analyze the results to identify areas for

improvement and enhance the application's resiliency.

Tools for Testing Serverless Applications

A variety of tools are available to support testing efforts in serverless applications. These tools can assist with unit testing, integration testing, performance testing, and more. Below are some popular testing tools for serverless environments.

1. Jest

Jest is a widely used testing framework for JavaScript applications. It provides a simple and intuitive API for writing unit tests and is especially popular for testing serverless functions built with Node.js.

- **Key Features**:
- Built-in mocking capabilities for isolating dependencies.
- Snapshot testing for capturing and comparing function output.
- Easy integration with CI/CD pipelines.

2. Mocha

Mocha is a flexible testing framework for Node.js that supports asynchronous testing. It is often used for unit testing serverless functions and offers extensive configuration options.

- **Key Features**:
- Support for multiple assertion libraries (e.g., Chai, Should.js).
- Customizable reporting options for test results.
- Support for testing asynchronous code with Promises and callbacks.

3. AWS SAM CLI

AWS SAM CLI (Serverless Application Model Command Line Interface) is a tool that simplifies the development and testing of serverless applications on AWS. It provides a local testing environment for AWS Lambda functions.

- **Key Features**:
- Local emulation of AWS services for testing serverless functions.
- Support for unit tests and integration tests.
- Simplified deployment to AWS for testing in the cloud.

4. Postman

Postman is a popular tool for testing APIs. It provides an intuitive interface for making API requests and validating responses, making it suitable for testing serverless APIs.

- **Key Features**:
- Ability to create and organize API requests in collections.
- Automated testing capabilities using scripts.
- Support for monitoring and documenting APIs.

5. Artillery

Artillery is a modern, powerful, and easy-to-use load testing tool for HTTP, WebSocket, and Socket.io applications. It is suitable for performance testing serverless applications.

- **Key Features**:
- Simple YAML-based configuration for defining load tests.
- Real-time reporting of test results.
- Support for testing APIs and microservices under load.

6. Snyk

Snyk is a security testing tool that helps identify vulnerabilities in application code and dependencies. It is essential for ensuring the security of serverless applications.

- **Key Features**:
- Continuous monitoring of open source dependencies for vulnerabilities.
- Integration with CI/CD pipelines for automated security checks.
- Remediation advice for fixing identified vulnerabilities.

Best Practices for Testing Serverless Applications

To ensure effective testing of serverless applications, organizations should follow best practices that align with their specific needs and goals. Below are key best practices for testing serverless applications:

1. Prioritize Automated Testing

Automation is critical for testing serverless applications efficiently. Implement automated testing processes that run tests continuously throughout the development lifecycle.

- **Continuous Integration**: Integrate automated tests into the CI/CD pipeline to ensure that tests are executed automatically whenever code changes are made.
- **Frequent Testing**: Run tests frequently to identify issues early in the development process. This reduces the cost of fixing bugs and enhances overall application quality.

2. Adopt a Testing Pyramid Approach

Utilize the testing pyramid approach to establish a balanced testing strategy. The testing pyramid consists of three layers: unit tests, integration tests, and end-to-end tests.

- **Unit Tests**: Focus on writing a high volume of unit tests to validate the functionality of individual serverless functions.
- **Integration Tests**: Use a moderate number of integration tests to verify interactions between services and components.
- **End-to-End Tests**: Limit the number of end-to-end tests, as they can be more complex and time-consuming to execute.

3. Implement Mocking and Stubbing

To effectively test serverless functions, utilize mocking and stubbing techniques to simulate external dependencies. This allows you to isolate the function's logic and avoid relying on external services during testing.

- **Mock External Services**: Use libraries (e.g., nock for Node.js) to mock external API calls and responses. This ensures that tests can run consistently without dependencies on real services.

4. Monitor Testing Metrics

Track testing metrics to assess the effectiveness of your testing efforts. Metrics such as test coverage, pass/fail rates, and execution times can provide valuable insights into the quality of your tests.

- **Set Coverage Targets**: Define coverage targets for unit tests to ensure that a significant portion of the codebase is tested. Monitor coverage trends over time to identify areas for improvement.

5. Continuously Review and Refine Tests

Regularly review and refine your testing practices to align with changes in the application and business requirements. As the application evolves, ensure that tests remain relevant and effective.

- **Refactor Tests**: Refactor tests to improve readability, maintainability, and performance. Remove or update outdated tests that no longer reflect the current application behavior.
- **Incorporate Feedback**: Gather feedback from development and testing teams to identify opportunities for improving testing practices.

6. Train Teams on Testing Best Practices

Educate development teams on testing best practices and the importance of thorough testing in serverless applications. Foster a culture of quality and collaboration to enhance overall testing efforts.

- **Conduct Workshops**: Organize workshops and training sessions on testing techniques, tools, and best practices. Encourage team members to share knowledge and experiences related to testing.

Conclusion

Testing is a vital component of building reliable and high-quality serverless applications. By implementing effective testing strategies, organizations can ensure that their applications function correctly, meet user expectations, and maintain a high level of quality.

This chapter explored various testing strategies, tools, and best practices for testing serverless applications. By prioritizing automated testing, adopting a testing pyramid approach, and continuously refining testing practices, organizations can enhance the reliability and performance of their serverless systems.

As we continue our exploration of serverless design patterns, we will delve into additional strategies and techniques for optimizing serverless applications, equipping you with the knowledge to navigate the complexities of modern software development.

Chapter 10: Debugging and Troubleshooting Serverless Applications

I n the fast-paced world of software development, ensuring the reliability and performance of applications is paramount. As organizations increasingly adopt serverless architectures, the need for effective debugging and troubleshooting practices has become even more critical. Serverless applications, while offering numerous advantages such as reduced operational overhead and scalability, also present unique challenges in diagnosing issues and resolving them promptly.

This chapter will delve into the essential aspects of debugging and troubleshooting in serverless applications, including common challenges, effective strategies, tools, and best practices. By equipping developers and operations teams with the knowledge and tools to effectively debug serverless applications, organizations can enhance their ability to maintain high-quality, reliable systems.

Understanding Debugging in Serverless Architectures

The Unique Nature of Serverless Debugging

Debugging serverless applications differs significantly from traditional monolithic or microservices architectures. The key differences include:

1. **Ephemeral Functions**: Serverless functions are stateless and ephemeral, meaning they do not retain context between invocations. This can make it challenging to trace the flow of execution and identify issues.

2. **Distributed Components**: Serverless applications often comprise multiple microservices that communicate over APIs and events. Debugging issues that span across multiple services can be complex and requires a comprehensive understanding of the application architecture.

3. **Limited Local Testing**: Local development environments for serverless functions may not accurately replicate the cloud environment, making it difficult to reproduce issues that occur in production.

4. **Event-Driven Architecture**: Many serverless applications are built using event-driven architectures, where services respond to events from various sources. This can introduce challenges in tracking the source of events and understanding how they propagate through the system.

Importance of Effective Debugging

Effective debugging is essential for several reasons:

1. **Rapid Issue Resolution**: Promptly identifying and resolving issues helps minimize downtime and maintain application availability. This is especially critical in production environments where user experience is impacted.

2. **Enhanced Code Quality**: Thorough debugging practices contribute to improved code quality by identifying defects early in the development process. This leads to more reliable applications and reduces the risk of issues in production.

108

3. **Increased Developer Productivity**: By streamlining the debugging process, developers can spend more time focusing on building new features and enhancing application functionality rather than troubleshooting issues.

4. **User Satisfaction**: Ensuring that applications function correctly and reliably leads to higher levels of user satisfaction. Effective debugging practices help maintain application performance and usability.

Common Challenges in Debugging Serverless Applications

Debugging serverless applications presents several challenges that teams must navigate to effectively identify and resolve issues. Understanding these challenges can help inform strategies for effective debugging.

1. Lack of Context

Since serverless functions are stateless, they do not retain information between invocations. This can make it difficult to understand the context in which an error occurred or to trace the flow of execution through multiple invocations.

2. Distributed Nature

Serverless applications often comprise multiple microservices that communicate over APIs and events. Debugging issues that span multiple services can be complex and require a comprehensive understanding of the interactions between components.

3. Limited Local Environment

Local development environments may not accurately replicate the cloud environment in which serverless functions run. This can make it challenging to reproduce issues that occur in production.

4. Event-Driven Complexity

In event-driven architectures, issues can arise from asynchronous events or delayed event processing. Understanding the sequence of events and their impact on the application can be challenging.

5. Cold Start Issues

Cold starts refer to the additional latency experienced when a serverless function is invoked after being idle. This can make it difficult to identify performance issues and understand how they impact user experience.

6. Logging Limitations

Logging is essential for debugging, but serverless functions may generate large volumes of logs. Filtering through extensive log data to identify relevant information can be time-consuming and challenging.

Strategies for Debugging Serverless Applications

To effectively debug serverless applications, teams should adopt a structured approach that incorporates various strategies and techniques. The following strategies can help streamline the debugging process and improve issue resolution.

1. Use Structured Logging

Structured logging involves logging messages in a consistent format that can be easily parsed and analyzed. This can significantly enhance the debugging process by making it easier to search for relevant log entries.

Best Practices for Structured Logging

- **Include Contextual Information**: Log messages should include relevant contextual information, such as function name, request ID, and user ID. This helps trace specific invocations and understand the context of errors.

- **Use JSON Format**: Consider logging messages in JSON format to facilitate easy parsing and filtering. JSON logs can be ingested by log analysis tools for more advanced querying and visualization.
- **Log at Appropriate Levels**: Use different log levels (e.g., debug, info, warn, error) to categorize log messages. This allows teams to filter logs based on severity and focus on relevant information.

2. Implement Distributed Tracing

Distributed tracing allows teams to visualize the flow of requests across multiple services, providing insights into performance bottlenecks and dependencies.

Key Steps for Implementing Distributed Tracing

- **Use Tracing Libraries**: Implement tracing libraries compatible with your serverless environment (e.g., AWS X-Ray, OpenTelemetry). These libraries automatically instrument your serverless functions to capture tracing data.
- **Propagate Trace Context**: Ensure that trace context (e.g., trace ID, span ID) is propagated across service boundaries. This allows for a comprehensive view of how requests traverse the application.
- **Analyze Trace Data**: Use tracing data to identify latency issues, service dependencies, and potential bottlenecks in the application. Visualizing trace data helps teams understand how different components interact.

3. Utilize Monitoring Tools

Monitoring tools provide insights into application performance and health, helping teams identify and diagnose issues proactively.

Key Features to Look for in Monitoring Tools

- **Real-Time Metrics**: Choose monitoring tools that provide real-time metrics on function execution, error rates, and response times. This allows teams to track application health continuously.
- **Custom Dashboards**: Use monitoring tools that allow for the creation of custom dashboards to visualize key metrics and performance indicators. Dashboards should be tailored to meet the needs of different stakeholders.
- **Alerting Mechanisms**: Implement alerting mechanisms to notify teams of critical issues or anomalies. Alerts should be actionable and provide context for troubleshooting.

4. Conduct Root Cause Analysis (RCA)

When issues arise, conducting root cause analysis helps identify the underlying factors contributing to the problem. RCA is a structured process that can lead to more effective solutions and prevent recurrence.

Steps for Conducting RCA

1. **Gather Data**: Collect relevant data, including logs, metrics, and traces, to understand the context of the issue. This helps build a comprehensive picture of what transpired.
2. **Identify Contributing Factors**: Analyze the collected data to identify contributing factors to the issue. Look for patterns, anomalies, and trends that may provide insights.
3. **Develop Hypotheses**: Formulate hypotheses about potential root causes based on the analysis. Consider different angles, such as code changes, configuration issues, or external service dependencies.
4. **Test Hypotheses**: Validate hypotheses through testing and experimentation. This may involve reproducing the issue in a controlled environment or analyzing additional data.
5. **Implement Solutions**: Once the root cause is identified, implement solutions to address the issue and prevent future occurrences.

5. Use Local Development and Testing Tools

Local development and testing tools can help replicate serverless environments and facilitate debugging during development.

Key Tools and Techniques

- **Local Emulation**: Use tools like AWS SAM CLI or Serverless Framework to emulate serverless functions locally. This allows for testing and debugging without deploying to the cloud.
- **Unit Testing Frameworks**: Implement unit testing frameworks (e.g., Jest, Mocha) to test individual serverless functions in isolation. This helps ensure that functions behave as expected before deployment.
- **Integration Testing**: Conduct integration tests in a staging environment that mirrors the production setup. This helps identify issues related to interactions between services.

6. Implement Error Handling and Fallback Mechanisms

Robust error handling and fallback mechanisms can enhance the resilience of serverless applications and improve the debugging process.

Best Practices for Error Handling

- **Graceful Error Handling**: Implement graceful error handling to manage exceptions effectively. This includes returning meaningful error messages and status codes to clients.
- **Fallback Strategies**: Use fallback strategies to provide alternative responses when a function fails. This helps maintain user experience even in the face of errors.
- **Log Errors**: Ensure that all errors are logged with sufficient context for debugging. Include relevant information, such as request details, error messages, and stack traces.

Tools for Debugging Serverless Applications

Several tools can assist developers and operations teams in debugging serverless applications. These tools provide capabilities for logging, monitoring, tracing, and testing. Below are some popular tools for debugging serverless applications.

1. AWS CloudWatch

AWS CloudWatch is a monitoring and observability service that provides logging, metrics, and event tracking for AWS resources, including serverless functions (AWS Lambda).

- **Key Features**:
- **CloudWatch Logs**: Centralized logging for AWS Lambda functions, allowing teams to search and analyze logs for troubleshooting.
- **CloudWatch Metrics**: Real-time metrics on function execution, error rates, and latency, enabling teams to monitor application health.

2. Azure Monitor

Azure Monitor is a comprehensive monitoring solution for applications running on Microsoft Azure. It provides insights into performance and resource utilization across Azure services, including serverless functions (Azure Functions).

- **Key Features**:
- **Application Insights**: Deep insights into application performance, user behavior, and exceptions, helping teams diagnose issues effectively.
- **Log Analytics**: Powerful querying and analysis capabilities for logs generated by Azure Functions.

3. Google Cloud Operations Suite

The **Google Cloud Operations Suite** (formerly Stackdriver) provides integrated monitoring, logging, and diagnostics for applications running on Google Cloud Platform (GCP).

- **Key Features**:
- **Stackdriver Logging**: Centralized logging capabilities for Google Cloud Functions, enabling easy access to logs for debugging.
- **Stackdriver Monitoring**: Real-time monitoring of performance metrics and resource utilization.

4. OpenTelemetry

OpenTelemetry is an open-source observability framework that provides APIs, libraries, and instrumentation for collecting metrics, logs, and traces.

- **Key Features**:
- **Distributed Tracing**: Allows teams to trace requests as they traverse multiple services, providing visibility into application behavior.
- **Language Support**: Supports multiple programming languages, allowing developers to instrument applications in their preferred language.

5. Sentry

Sentry is an error tracking tool that helps developers monitor and fix crashes in real-time. It provides detailed error reports and context for debugging.

- **Key Features**:
- **Real-Time Alerts**: Notifications for errors and exceptions, allowing teams to respond quickly to issues.
- **Contextual Information**: Provides detailed context for errors, including stack traces, user actions, and environment data.

6. Postman

Postman is a popular tool for testing APIs and can also be used for debugging serverless functions exposed via APIs.

- **Key Features**:
- **API Testing**: Allows users to make requests to serverless APIs and validate responses, helping to identify issues with endpoints.
- **Automated Testing**: Supports automated testing and monitoring of API behavior.

Best Practices for Debugging Serverless Applications

To ensure effective debugging of serverless applications, organizations should adhere to the following best practices:

1. Embrace a Culture of Observability

Encourage a culture of observability within development and operations teams. This involves prioritizing monitoring and observability practices as part of the application development lifecycle.

- **Education and Training**: Provide training on observability concepts and tools to empower teams to implement effective monitoring and debugging practices.

2. Document Debugging Processes

Create comprehensive documentation outlining debugging processes, tools, and best practices. This ensures that team members have access to relevant information and can troubleshoot issues efficiently.

- **Knowledge Sharing**: Foster a culture of knowledge sharing by documenting lessons learned from debugging experiences and sharing them across teams.

3. Use Version Control for Infrastructure

Use version control systems (e.g., Git) to manage infrastructure as code (IaC) for serverless applications. This allows teams to track changes, roll back configurations, and maintain consistency.

- **Infrastructure Automation**: Automate the deployment of serverless functions and associated resources using IaC tools (e.g., AWS CloudFormation, Azure Resource Manager).

4. Regularly Review Logging Practices

Periodically review logging practices to ensure they align with the needs of the development and operations teams. This includes assessing log formats, levels, and retention policies.

- **Log Retention Policies**: Define log retention policies to balance the need for historical data with storage costs.

5. Encourage Cross-Team Collaboration

Foster collaboration between development and operations teams to enhance debugging efforts. Encourage teams to work together on debugging issues and share insights.

- **Blameless Postmortems**: Conduct blameless postmortems after incidents to analyze the root cause of issues and identify areas for improvement without assigning blame.

6. Continuously Improve Debugging Practices

Debugging practices should evolve as applications change and new challenges arise. Regularly assess the effectiveness of debugging strategies and make adjustments as needed.

- **Feedback Loop**: Establish feedback loops to gather input from teams on debugging practices and incorporate their suggestions for improvement.

Conclusion

Debugging and troubleshooting serverless applications are critical for maintaining reliability, performance, and user satisfaction. By adopting effective strategies, utilizing the right tools, and following best practices, organizations can enhance their ability to diagnose and resolve issues in serverless environments.

This chapter explored the unique challenges of debugging serverless applications, strategies for effective debugging, and tools that can assist in the process. By prioritizing observability, implementing structured logging, leveraging distributed tracing, and fostering a culture of collaboration, teams can significantly improve their debugging efforts.

As we continue to explore serverless design patterns and best practices, the knowledge gained from this chapter will empower organizations to navigate the complexities of debugging in modern software development, ensuring the successful delivery of high-quality, reliable serverless applications.

Chapter 11: Best Practices for Deployment in Serverless Applications

A s organizations transition to serverless architectures, the deployment process becomes a critical aspect of application development. Serverless computing offers a variety of benefits, including automatic scaling, reduced operational overhead, and cost-effectiveness, but it also introduces unique challenges in deploying and managing applications. Effective deployment practices are essential for ensuring the reliability, performance, and security of serverless applications.

This chapter will explore best practices for deploying serverless applications, covering deployment strategies, tools, and techniques that can enhance the deployment process. By implementing these best practices, organizations can ensure smooth, efficient, and reliable deployments of their serverless systems.

Understanding Deployment in Serverless Architectures

The Unique Nature of Serverless Deployment

Deploying serverless applications differs significantly from traditional deployment processes. Key differences include:

1. **Ephemeral Functions**: Serverless functions are stateless and short-lived, which means they are created and destroyed on demand. This requires careful management of function versions and configuration settings.

2. **Microservices Architecture**: Serverless applications are often composed of multiple microservices that interact with each other. This necessitates coordination among services during deployment to ensure compatibility and functionality.

3. **Event-Driven Communication**: Many serverless applications rely on events to trigger functions. Ensuring that event sources and consumers are correctly configured is critical for successful deployments.

4. **Cloud Provider Dependencies**: Deployment processes are often tied to specific cloud providers and their tools, requiring teams to be familiar with the nuances of each platform.

Importance of Effective Deployment Practices

Effective deployment practices are essential for several reasons:

1. **Minimize Downtime**: A well-defined deployment process can help minimize downtime during updates and ensure that applications remain available to users.

2. **Enhance Reliability**: By following best practices for deployment, organizations can reduce the risk of introducing bugs or breaking changes that could impact application reliability.

3. **Improve Developer Efficiency**: Streamlined deployment processes enable development teams to deploy updates quickly and efficiently, allowing them to focus on building new features rather than managing deployment challenges.

4. **Facilitate Rollbacks**: In the event of deployment failures, effective practices ensure that rollbacks can be performed quickly and easily to restore application functionality.

Deployment Strategies for Serverless Applications

Several deployment strategies can be employed to ensure successful deployments of serverless applications. These strategies encompass approaches like blue-green deployments, canary releases, and rolling updates. Each strategy has its own advantages and considerations.

1. Blue-Green Deployments

Blue-green deployments involve maintaining two separate environments: the "blue" environment, which is the current production environment, and the "green" environment, where the new version of the application is deployed. This strategy allows for a seamless transition between versions.

Key Steps for Blue-Green Deployments

1. **Set Up Two Environments**: Create two identical environments, labeled blue and green. The blue environment is the active production environment, while the green environment is used for testing and deploying new features.
2. **Deploy to the Green Environment**: Deploy the new version of the application to the green environment. Conduct testing and validation to ensure that the application behaves as expected.
3. **Switch Traffic**: Once the green environment is validated, switch traffic from the blue environment to the green environment. This can be done through load balancers or DNS updates.
4. **Monitor and Rollback**: Monitor the green environment for issues. If problems arise, traffic can be quickly switched back to the blue environment, minimizing downtime.

Advantages of Blue-Green Deployments

- **Reduced Downtime**: The switch between environments is typically instantaneous, minimizing user disruption during deployments.
- **Easy Rollback**: If issues are detected in the green environment, rolling back to the blue environment is straightforward and quick.

Considerations

- **Resource Costs**: Maintaining two environments can be resource-intensive and may incur additional costs.
- **Complexity**: Setting up and managing blue-green deployments may introduce complexity, particularly for larger applications.

2. Canary Releases

Canary releases involve deploying a new version of the application to a small subset of users or traffic before rolling it out to the entire user base. This strategy allows teams to test new features and monitor their performance with minimal risk.

Key Steps for Canary Releases

1. **Deploy to a Subset of Users**: Deploy the new version of the application to a small percentage of users (e.g., 5% or 10%). This can be achieved through feature flags or traffic routing.
2. **Monitor Performance**: Monitor the performance of the canary release for issues, such as errors or degraded user experience. This helps teams identify potential problems early.
3. **Gradual Rollout**: If the canary release is successful, gradually increase the percentage of users receiving the new version until it is fully deployed to all users.
4. **Rollback if Necessary**: If significant issues are detected during the canary release, the deployment can be rolled back for the affected users

without impacting the entire user base.

Advantages of Canary Releases

- **Reduced Risk**: By limiting exposure to a small subset of users, teams can mitigate the risk associated with introducing new features.
- **Real-World Testing**: Canary releases allow teams to test new features in a real-world environment and gather valuable feedback from users.

Considerations

- **Complexity in Management**: Managing different versions of the application and routing traffic can add complexity to deployment processes.
- **Data Integrity**: Ensuring that data is consistent between the canary and production environments can be challenging.

3. Rolling Updates

Rolling updates involve incrementally updating instances of the application in a controlled manner. In a serverless context, this typically means deploying new versions of functions gradually rather than all at once.

Key Steps for Rolling Updates

1. **Deploy in Batches**: Deploy the new version of the serverless function in small batches (e.g., a few instances at a time) rather than updating all instances simultaneously.
2. **Monitor Performance**: Continuously monitor the performance and health of the updated instances. If issues are detected, the update can be paused or rolled back.
3. **Complete the Rollout**: Once the updated instances are validated, continue rolling out the new version to the remaining instances until the entire application is updated.

Advantages of Rolling Updates

- **Reduced Impact**: By updating in small batches, the impact of potential issues is minimized, allowing for quicker identification and resolution of problems.
- **Continuous Availability**: The application remains available throughout the update process, ensuring minimal disruption for users.

Considerations

- **Complexity**: Managing multiple versions of functions during the rollout can introduce complexity in monitoring and troubleshooting.
- **Testing Requirements**: Thorough testing is required before initiating rolling updates to ensure that the new version is stable.

Tools for Deployment in Serverless Applications

Several tools can assist with the deployment of serverless applications, providing capabilities for managing infrastructure, automating deployments, and monitoring application performance. Below are some popular deployment tools for serverless environments.

1. AWS SAM CLI

AWS Serverless Application Model (SAM) CLI is a command-line interface for building, testing, and deploying serverless applications on AWS.

- **Key Features**:
- Local testing and debugging capabilities for AWS Lambda functions.
- Simplified deployment of serverless applications using AWS CloudFormation.
- Integration with AWS CodePipeline for CI/CD automation.

2. Serverless Framework

The **Serverless Framework** is an open-source framework that simplifies the deployment and management of serverless applications across various cloud providers.

- **Key Features**:
- Multi-cloud support, allowing deployment to AWS, Azure, Google Cloud, and more.
- Infrastructure as Code (IaC) capabilities for managing resources and functions.
- Support for plugins to extend functionality and customize workflows.

3. AWS CloudFormation

AWS CloudFormation is a service that provides a way to model and set up AWS resources using code. It enables teams to define infrastructure as code for serverless applications.

- **Key Features**:
- Version control for infrastructure resources, enabling easy updates and rollbacks.
- Automated provisioning of AWS resources based on templates.
- Integration with AWS services for seamless deployments.

4. Azure Resource Manager (ARM)

Azure Resource Manager (ARM) is the deployment and management service for Azure that allows users to create, update, and delete resources in their Azure environment.

- **Key Features**:
- Infrastructure as Code capabilities for defining and managing Azure

resources.

- Support for templates to automate deployments of serverless applications.
- Role-based access control for managing resource permissions.

5. Google Cloud Deployment Manager

Google Cloud Deployment Manager is an infrastructure as code service that allows users to create, configure, and deploy Google Cloud resources.

- **Key Features**:
- Declarative configuration files for managing cloud resources.
- Integration with Google Cloud services for seamless deployments.
- Support for templates and modules to reuse configurations.

Best Practices for Deploying Serverless Applications

To ensure effective deployment of serverless applications, organizations should adhere to the following best practices:

1. Adopt Infrastructure as Code (IaC)

Utilizing infrastructure as code allows teams to define and manage serverless resources programmatically. This approach provides several benefits, including version control, consistency, and automation.

- **Version Control**: Store IaC templates in version control systems (e.g., Git) to track changes and facilitate collaboration.
- **Automated Provisioning**: Use IaC tools (e.g., AWS CloudFormation, Serverless Framework) to automate the provisioning of serverless resources, reducing manual errors.

2. Implement CI/CD Pipelines

Continuous integration and continuous deployment (CI/CD) pipelines automate the deployment process, ensuring that updates are delivered efficiently and reliably.

- **Automated Testing**: Integrate automated testing into the CI/CD pipeline to validate application functionality and performance before deployment.
- **Deployment Automation**: Use deployment tools to automate the deployment of serverless functions and associated resources, reducing the risk of manual errors.

3. Maintain Versioning

Versioning is essential for managing updates to serverless functions. By implementing versioning practices, organizations can track changes and manage releases effectively.

- **Use Function Versions**: Utilize versioning features provided by cloud platforms (e.g., AWS Lambda versioning) to maintain different versions of serverless functions.
- **Semantic Versioning**: Adopt semantic versioning conventions to communicate the nature of changes (e.g., major, minor, patch) clearly.

4. Monitor and Measure Deployments

Monitoring deployment metrics is crucial for assessing the success of deployments and identifying potential issues.

- **Track Deployment Metrics**: Monitor metrics such as deployment success rates, error rates, and performance impact during and after deployments.

- **Set Up Alerts**: Configure alerts for critical deployment metrics to notify teams of issues that require immediate attention.

5. Implement Rollback Strategies

Having rollback strategies in place is essential for mitigating risks associated with deployments.

- **Automated Rollbacks**: Implement automated rollback mechanisms to revert to previous versions in case of deployment failures or issues.
- **Test Rollback Procedures**: Regularly test rollback procedures to ensure that they are effective and can be executed quickly when needed.

6. Keep Dependencies Updated

Regularly updating dependencies is crucial for maintaining security and performance in serverless applications.

- **Dependency Management**: Use dependency management tools (e.g., npm, pip) to track and update third-party libraries and packages.
- **Security Scanning**: Implement security scanning tools to identify vulnerabilities in dependencies and apply updates promptly.

7. Conduct Post-Deployment Reviews

Conducting post-deployment reviews helps teams assess the effectiveness of deployment practices and identify areas for improvement.

- **Gather Feedback**: Solicit feedback from development and operations teams on the deployment process and any challenges encountered.
- **Document Lessons Learned**: Document lessons learned and best practices for future deployments, fostering a culture of continuous improvement.

Conclusion

Effective deployment practices are essential for the success of serverless applications. By adopting strategies such as blue-green deployments, canary releases, and rolling updates, organizations can minimize downtime, enhance reliability, and improve developer efficiency.

This chapter explored various deployment strategies, tools, and best practices for deploying serverless applications. By implementing infrastructure as code, establishing CI/CD pipelines, and maintaining versioning, organizations can streamline their deployment processes and ensure smooth, reliable updates.

As we continue to explore serverless design patterns and best practices, the knowledge gained from this chapter will empower organizations to navigate the complexities of deploying serverless applications, ensuring the successful delivery of high-quality, reliable systems in today's dynamic software development landscape.

Chapter 12: Case Studies of Successful Serverless Applications

I n recent years, serverless computing has emerged as a transformative architecture for building and deploying applications. Organizations across various industries are leveraging the benefits of serverless technology to enhance agility, reduce costs, and improve scalability. This chapter explores several case studies of successful serverless applications, highlighting how different organizations have implemented serverless architectures, the challenges they faced, and the results they achieved. These real-world examples will provide valuable insights into the practical applications of serverless computing and serve as inspiration for organizations considering similar transitions.

Case Study 1: Coca-Cola - Optimizing Customer Engagement

Background

Coca-Cola is one of the world's leading beverage companies, with a vast portfolio of products and a global presence. The company has a strong focus on customer engagement and leveraging data analytics to enhance its marketing efforts. To optimize its customer engagement initiatives, Coca-Cola sought a scalable, cost-effective solution that could handle high traffic during promotional campaigns and events.

Challenge

Coca-Cola faced challenges with its traditional web applications, which struggled to handle sudden spikes in traffic during marketing campaigns and product launches. The company needed a solution that could scale automatically, reduce latency, and lower operational costs.

Solution

Coca-Cola adopted a serverless architecture to power its customer engagement platform. The company implemented AWS Lambda functions to handle API requests, process user interactions, and manage data analytics. By leveraging Amazon API Gateway, Coca-Cola was able to create a secure and scalable API layer for its applications.

- **Event-Driven Architecture**: Coca-Cola utilized event-driven architecture, allowing functions to be triggered by specific events, such as user interactions or promotional campaigns.
- **Data Analytics**: AWS Lambda was used to process large volumes of data from customer interactions, enabling real-time analytics and insights.

Results

The implementation of a serverless architecture enabled Coca-Cola to achieve the following results:

- **Scalability**: The serverless solution automatically scaled to handle millions of requests during peak traffic periods, ensuring a seamless user experience.
- **Cost Reduction**: By only paying for actual usage, Coca-Cola significantly reduced infrastructure costs compared to traditional hosting solutions.

- **Faster Time to Market**: The company was able to deploy new features and campaigns rapidly, enhancing its ability to engage with customers effectively.

Lessons Learned

Coca-Cola's experience highlights the importance of:

- **Leveraging Cloud Services**: Using managed cloud services can simplify infrastructure management and reduce operational overhead.
- **Event-Driven Design**: An event-driven architecture allows for flexibility and scalability, making it easier to respond to changing business needs.

Case Study 2: Netflix - Enhancing Streaming Services

Background

Netflix is a global leader in streaming entertainment, with millions of subscribers accessing content from various devices. To maintain its position as a market leader, Netflix continually seeks ways to enhance the user experience, improve performance, and reduce costs.

Challenge

Netflix faced challenges in managing its infrastructure and ensuring high availability during peak viewing times. The traditional architecture required significant resources to manage and scale, leading to high operational costs and complexity.

Solution

Netflix adopted a serverless approach for specific components of its architecture, particularly for handling backend processes and data processing tasks.

- **AWS Lambda for Data Processing**: Netflix leveraged AWS Lambda to process data generated by user interactions and streaming activities. This included tasks such as logging, analytics, and recommendation engine computations.
- **Microservices Architecture**: By breaking down applications into microservices, Netflix could deploy individual components independently, enhancing flexibility and scalability.

Results

The transition to a serverless architecture yielded significant benefits for Netflix:

- **Improved Scalability**: AWS Lambda automatically scaled to handle varying workloads, allowing Netflix to accommodate fluctuations in user demand without overprovisioning resources.
- **Cost Efficiency**: By utilizing serverless functions for specific tasks, Netflix reduced infrastructure costs and improved resource utilization.
- **Faster Development Cycles**: The microservices approach enabled faster development and deployment of new features, enhancing the overall user experience.

Lessons Learned

Netflix's journey emphasizes the importance of:

- **Microservices Design**: Adopting a microservices architecture can improve agility and allow teams to innovate quickly.

- **Data-Driven Decisions**: Leveraging data processing capabilities in a serverless environment enables real-time insights and better user engagement.

Case Study 3: The BBC - Streamlining Content Delivery

Background

The British Broadcasting Corporation (BBC) is a public service broadcaster in the UK, providing a wide range of content, including news, entertainment, and educational programming. With a growing digital audience, the BBC sought to enhance its content delivery and improve the performance of its digital services.

Challenge

The BBC faced challenges in delivering content to millions of users, particularly during peak events such as major sporting competitions and news broadcasts. The traditional infrastructure struggled to scale effectively, leading to performance issues and user dissatisfaction.

Solution

The BBC implemented a serverless architecture to streamline its content delivery processes. This included utilizing AWS Lambda for processing and delivering media content.

- **Content Processing**: AWS Lambda was used to process and encode video content, enabling faster delivery and improved performance.
- **Event-Driven Content Delivery**: The BBC adopted an event-driven approach, where content delivery functions were triggered by specific events, such as new content uploads or user requests.

Results

The serverless implementation enabled the BBC to achieve several key outcomes:

- **Enhanced Performance**: The BBC significantly improved content delivery speed, resulting in a better user experience during peak viewing times.
- **Scalability**: The serverless architecture allowed the BBC to scale automatically in response to traffic spikes, ensuring reliable service availability.
- **Cost Savings**: By transitioning to a serverless model, the BBC reduced operational costs associated with managing traditional infrastructure.

Lessons Learned

The BBC's experience illustrates the importance of:

- **User-Centric Design**: Focusing on user experience and performance can lead to increased audience engagement and satisfaction.
- **Scalable Solutions**: Implementing scalable solutions is crucial for managing traffic fluctuations and ensuring service reliability.

Case Study 4: AirAsia - Transforming Customer Experience

Background

AirAsia is a leading low-cost airline in Asia, known for its innovative approach to travel and customer service. With a focus on enhancing the customer experience, AirAsia sought to modernize its digital services and improve operational efficiency.

Challenge

AirAsia faced challenges in managing its booking and customer service systems, which struggled to handle high volumes of inquiries and bookings during peak travel periods. The existing infrastructure was costly and complex to manage.

Solution

AirAsia adopted a serverless architecture to streamline its booking and customer service processes. By leveraging AWS Lambda and other serverless technologies, the airline was able to modernize its systems.

- **Serverless Booking System**: The airline developed a serverless booking system that utilized AWS Lambda functions to handle user requests and process transactions.
- **Chatbot Integration**: AirAsia integrated serverless functions with a chatbot to provide instant customer support and improve response times.

Results

The transition to a serverless architecture yielded significant benefits for AirAsia:

- **Improved Customer Experience**: The airline significantly enhanced its booking and customer service processes, leading to higher customer satisfaction ratings.
- **Cost Efficiency**: By reducing operational costs associated with traditional infrastructure, AirAsia was able to allocate resources toward improving customer-facing initiatives.
- **Scalability**: The serverless architecture allowed AirAsia to scale automatically during peak travel seasons, ensuring a seamless user experience.

Lessons Learned

AirAsia's experience underscores the importance of:

- **Innovative Solutions**: Embracing innovative technologies can drive significant improvements in customer experience and operational efficiency.
- **Adaptability**: The ability to adapt to changing customer needs and market conditions is crucial for success in the competitive airline industry.

Case Study 5: iRobot - Enhancing Product Connectivity

Background

iRobot is a leading company in consumer robotics, known for its popular Roomba robotic vacuum cleaners. With a growing focus on connected devices, iRobot sought to enhance the connectivity and functionality of its products.

Challenge

As iRobot expanded its product offerings, the company faced challenges in managing the connectivity and data processing requirements of its devices. Traditional infrastructure was costly and difficult to scale to meet the demands of a growing user base.

Solution

iRobot implemented a serverless architecture to enhance the connectivity of its devices and improve data processing capabilities. The company leveraged AWS Lambda to handle events generated by its connected devices.

- **Event-Driven Architecture**: iRobot adopted an event-driven architecture, where serverless functions were triggered by events from connected devices, such as user interactions or status updates.
- **Real-Time Data Processing**: AWS Lambda was used to process data collected from devices in real-time, enabling actionable insights and improved user experiences.

Results

The implementation of a serverless architecture enabled iRobot to achieve several key outcomes:

- **Improved Device Connectivity**: iRobot significantly enhanced the connectivity of its devices, allowing for seamless integration with mobile applications and smart home ecosystems.
- **Scalable Data Processing**: The serverless architecture allowed iRobot to process large volumes of data from connected devices without incurring significant infrastructure costs.
- **Enhanced User Experience**: The ability to provide real-time insights and notifications improved the overall user experience for iRobot customers.

Lessons Learned

iRobot's experience highlights the importance of:

- **Connectivity in IoT**: Ensuring seamless connectivity is critical for the success of IoT devices and enhancing user engagement.
- **Real-Time Data Processing**: The ability to process data in real-time can lead to valuable insights and improve overall product functionality.

Conclusion

The case studies presented in this chapter illustrate the transformative impact of serverless computing across various industries. Organizations such as Coca-Cola, Netflix, the BBC, AirAsia, and iRobot have successfully leveraged serverless architectures to enhance scalability, improve performance, and optimize costs.

By understanding the unique challenges and advantages of serverless computing, organizations can make informed decisions about adopting serverless architectures for their applications. These real-world examples serve as valuable insights into the practical applications of serverless technology and demonstrate how it can drive innovation, improve customer experiences, and enhance operational efficiency.

As organizations continue to explore the potential of serverless computing, the knowledge gained from these case studies can inform their strategies, helping them navigate the complexities of building and deploying serverless applications successfully. The journey toward serverless architecture may present challenges, but the potential rewards make it a compelling option for organizations seeking to stay competitive in today's fast-paced digital landscape.

Chapter 13: Future Trends and Innovations in Serverless Computing

S erverless computing has revolutionized the way developers build and deploy applications. As technology evolves, serverless architectures continue to gain traction across various industries, providing organizations with unprecedented agility, scalability, and cost efficiency. In this chapter, we will explore the future trends and innovations shaping the serverless landscape, examining how advancements in technology, changes in development practices, and emerging use cases are set to redefine serverless computing.

The Growing Adoption of Serverless Computing

Increased Adoption Across Industries

The adoption of serverless computing has grown significantly over the past few years. Organizations in sectors ranging from finance to healthcare to entertainment are recognizing the benefits of serverless architectures, leading to a broader acceptance of this paradigm.

- **Cost Efficiency**: Serverless computing offers a pay-as-you-go pricing model, allowing organizations to only pay for actual usage. This can lead to significant cost savings compared to traditional infrastructure models, especially for applications with variable workloads.

- **Agility and Speed**: Serverless architectures enable developers to deploy applications faster, reducing time to market. This agility is particularly valuable in today's competitive landscape, where organizations must respond quickly to changing customer demands.

The Rise of Hybrid Architectures

As organizations embrace serverless computing, many are adopting hybrid architectures that combine serverless functions with traditional server-based applications. This approach allows organizations to leverage the benefits of both models, optimizing performance, scalability, and cost.

- **Seamless Integration**: Hybrid architectures enable organizations to integrate existing applications with serverless components. For example, a company may use serverless functions to handle specific workloads while maintaining a traditional monolithic application for core functionality.
- **Gradual Migration**: Adopting a hybrid approach allows organizations to gradually migrate to serverless architectures without needing to overhaul existing systems. This can reduce risk and minimize disruption during the transition.

Innovations in Serverless Technologies

1. Improved Cold Start Performance

Cold starts are a common challenge in serverless computing, where the first invocation of a function incurs additional latency due to the initialization of resources. To address this issue, cloud providers are investing in technologies to improve cold start performance.

- **Provisioned Concurrency**: Some cloud providers, such as AWS

Lambda, offer provisioned concurrency, allowing users to pre-warm a certain number of function instances. This ensures that functions are ready to respond to incoming requests without incurring cold start latency.

- **Optimized Runtime Environments**: Cloud providers are continually optimizing runtime environments for serverless functions, reducing initialization times and improving performance. Innovations in container technology and function packaging can also contribute to faster cold start performance.

2. Enhanced Developer Tools and Frameworks

The development experience is a key factor in the adoption of serverless computing. As serverless architectures become more prevalent, developers are seeking tools and frameworks that simplify the development, testing, and deployment processes.

- **Serverless Frameworks**: Open-source frameworks such as the Serverless Framework, AWS SAM, and Azure Functions provide abstractions and tools that streamline serverless development. These frameworks enable developers to define resources, manage deployments, and automate testing with minimal effort.
- **Local Development Tools**: Tools that facilitate local development and testing of serverless functions are gaining popularity. Local emulation environments enable developers to run and test functions on their machines, reducing the need for constant deployment to the cloud during development.

3. Event-Driven Architectures

The adoption of event-driven architectures is becoming increasingly common in serverless computing. This approach allows developers to build applications that respond to events in real-time, enhancing interactivity and responsiveness.

- **Event Streaming**: Technologies like Apache Kafka, Amazon Kinesis, and Google Cloud Pub/Sub are facilitating event-driven architectures, enabling organizations to process streams of events in real-time. This is particularly valuable for applications that require real-time analytics or user interactions.
- **Microservices Integration**: Event-driven architectures allow for seamless integration between microservices in serverless applications. Services can publish and subscribe to events, enabling loose coupling and scalability.

4. Multi-Cloud Strategies

As organizations seek to avoid vendor lock-in and enhance resilience, multi-cloud strategies are becoming increasingly popular in the serverless space. By leveraging multiple cloud providers, organizations can optimize performance, cost, and availability.

- **Interoperability**: Multi-cloud architectures require interoperability between different cloud providers. As serverless technologies evolve, tools and frameworks that support cross-cloud deployments will become essential.
- **Data Management**: Managing data across multiple cloud providers presents challenges. Innovations in data synchronization and integration will be critical to ensure that serverless applications can access and process data seamlessly across environments.

Emerging Use Cases for Serverless Computing

1. Internet of Things (IoT) Applications

The Internet of Things (IoT) is a rapidly growing field that generates massive amounts of data from connected devices. Serverless computing is well-suited to handle the unique demands of IoT applications.

- **Event-Driven Processing**: Serverless architectures enable real-time processing of events generated by IoT devices. Functions can be triggered by incoming data streams, allowing organizations to analyze and respond to events in real-time.
- **Scalability**: Serverless computing can automatically scale to accommodate the varying workloads generated by IoT devices. This ensures that applications can handle spikes in traffic without manual intervention.

2. Machine Learning and AI

Serverless computing is being increasingly integrated into machine learning and artificial intelligence workflows. Organizations can leverage serverless functions to process data, train models, and deploy AI applications.

- **Data Preprocessing**: Serverless functions can be used to preprocess large datasets, transforming and cleaning data for machine learning applications. This allows organizations to streamline the data preparation process.
- **Model Deployment**: Deploying machine learning models as serverless functions enables organizations to make predictions on demand. This reduces infrastructure costs and simplifies the deployment process.

3. Real-Time Data Processing

Real-time data processing is essential for applications that require immediate insights and actions. Serverless architectures provide the scalability and responsiveness needed for real-time analytics.

- **Stream Processing**: Serverless functions can be used to process data streams from sources such as IoT devices, social media, and transaction logs. This allows organizations to analyze data in real-time and respond to changes quickly.
- **Data Transformation**: Serverless computing can facilitate data transformation and enrichment in real-time, enabling organizations to derive valuable insights from incoming data.

4. Web and Mobile Applications

Serverless architectures are increasingly being adopted for web and mobile applications due to their scalability and cost-effectiveness.

- **Backend Services**: Serverless functions can be used to build backend services for web and mobile applications, handling tasks such as user authentication, data storage, and business logic.
- **Static Site Hosting**: Many organizations are using serverless architectures to host static websites, taking advantage of services like AWS S3, Azure Blob Storage, and Netlify to deliver content efficiently.

Security Trends in Serverless Computing

1. Enhanced Security Features

As serverless computing gains popularity, cloud providers are investing in enhanced security features to protect serverless applications.

- **Built-in Security Controls**: Serverless platforms are integrating security controls such as API security, authentication, and access management directly into the deployment process. This helps organizations implement security best practices more easily.
- **Automated Vulnerability Scanning**: Automated tools for scanning serverless applications for vulnerabilities are becoming more common.

These tools can help identify security weaknesses in functions and dependencies.

2. Focus on Secure Development Practices

The shift to serverless architectures necessitates a renewed focus on secure development practices. Organizations must prioritize security throughout the development lifecycle.

- **Shift-Left Security**: Integrating security practices early in the development process helps identify and mitigate vulnerabilities before they reach production. This includes implementing security testing in CI/CD pipelines.
- **Security Awareness Training**: Training developers on secure coding practices and the specific security considerations of serverless architectures is essential for maintaining a strong security posture.

The Role of Edge Computing

1. Combining Serverless with Edge Computing

The convergence of serverless computing and edge computing is creating new opportunities for organizations to enhance performance and user experience.

- **Reduced Latency**: By deploying serverless functions at the edge, organizations can reduce latency and improve response times for users located far from central data centers.
- **Real-Time Processing**: Edge computing enables real-time data processing closer to the source, allowing organizations to make immediate decisions based on incoming data.

2. Use Cases for Serverless at the Edge

- **Content Delivery**: Serverless functions deployed at edge locations can be used to deliver content quickly and efficiently, enhancing the user experience for applications that require low latency.
- **IoT Edge Processing**: Organizations can leverage serverless functions at the edge to process data from IoT devices locally, reducing the need for data to be sent to central servers for processing.

Conclusion

The future of serverless computing is bright, with continued growth and innovation shaping the landscape. Organizations across various industries are recognizing the benefits of serverless architectures and adopting them to enhance agility, scalability, and cost-effectiveness.

In this chapter, we explored emerging trends and innovations in serverless computing, including the growing adoption of serverless architectures, advancements in technologies, and new use cases. By understanding these trends, organizations can position themselves for success in an increasingly competitive digital landscape.

As serverless computing continues to evolve, organizations that embrace these innovations and adapt their strategies will be well-equipped to navigate the complexities of modern software development and drive meaningful results. The insights gained from this chapter can serve as a roadmap for organizations seeking to leverage the full potential of serverless architectures in the years to come.

Chapter 14: Building a Complete Full-Stack Application with Serverless Architecture

I n today's software development landscape, building full-stack applications has evolved significantly. The combination of front-end and
back-end technologies has become increasingly streamlined through
the adoption of serverless architecture. This chapter will provide a
comprehensive guide to building a complete full-stack application using
serverless technologies, covering the necessary components, best practices,
and implementation details.

Understanding Full-Stack Development

Definition of Full-Stack Development

Full-stack development refers to the practice of developing both the front-
end (client side) and back-end (server side) of an application. A full-stack
developer is equipped with the skills to work on all layers of the application
stack, from user interfaces to databases.

Components of a Full-Stack Application

1. **Front-End**: This is the user interface (UI) that users interact with. It is typically built using technologies like HTML, CSS, and JavaScript frameworks such as React, Angular, or Vue.js.
2. **Back-End**: The back-end includes the server, application logic, and database. This is where data processing occurs, and it is often built using server-side languages like Node.js, Python, or Java.
3. **Database**: Databases are used to store application data. They can be relational (e.g., MySQL, PostgreSQL) or non-relational (e.g., MongoDB, DynamoDB).
4. **APIs**: Application Programming Interfaces (APIs) facilitate communication between the front-end and back-end. RESTful APIs or GraphQL are commonly used for this purpose.
5. **Cloud Services**: These services provide scalable infrastructure and resources for hosting applications, databases, and other components. Serverless computing services, such as AWS Lambda, Azure Functions, and Google Cloud Functions, are becoming increasingly popular for building back-end logic.

Why Choose Serverless Architecture for Full-Stack Development?

Benefits of Serverless Architecture

1. **Scalability**: Serverless architectures automatically scale to accommodate varying workloads, allowing applications to handle spikes in traffic without manual intervention.
2. **Cost Efficiency**: With a pay-as-you-go pricing model, organizations only pay for the actual usage of functions, which can significantly reduce infrastructure costs.
3. **Reduced Operational Overhead**: Serverless computing abstracts away infrastructure management tasks, enabling developers to focus on

writing code and delivering features.

4. **Faster Development**: Serverless architectures streamline the development process by allowing teams to quickly deploy and iterate on applications.

5. **Improved Resilience**: Many serverless platforms offer built-in fault tolerance and high availability, making it easier to build resilient applications.

Building a Complete Full-Stack Serverless Application

This section will guide you through the process of building a complete full-stack serverless application step by step. For this example, we will create a simple task management application that allows users to create, read, update, and delete (CRUD) tasks.

1. Defining the Application Requirements

Before diving into development, it's essential to define the requirements of the application:

- **User Authentication**: Users should be able to register, log in, and manage their sessions.
- **Task Management**: Users should be able to create, read, update, and delete tasks.
- **Data Storage**: Task data should be stored in a cloud database.
- **User Interface**: A user-friendly interface for managing tasks.

2. Choosing the Technology Stack

For this task management application, we will use the following technologies:

- **Front-End**: React.js for building the user interface.
- **Back-End**: AWS Lambda for serverless functions to handle API requests.

- **Database**: Amazon DynamoDB for storing task data.
- **Authentication**: AWS Cognito for user authentication.
- **API Gateway**: AWS API Gateway to manage API endpoints.

3. Setting Up the Development Environment

To get started, you need to set up your development environment with the necessary tools and libraries:

1. **Node.js**: Ensure that Node.js is installed on your machine. You can download it from the Node.js website.
2. **React Application**: Create a new React application using Create React App:

```bash
Copy code
npx create-react-app task-manager
cd task-manager
```

1. **AWS CLI**: Install the AWS Command Line Interface (CLI) to interact with AWS services:

```bash
Copy code
pip install awscli
```

1. **AWS SDK**: Install the AWS SDK for JavaScript to interact with AWS services from the front end:

```bash
Copy code
npm install aws-sdk
```

4. Setting Up AWS Services

a. Creating an AWS Account

If you don't already have an AWS account, you can create one at the AWS website. Once your account is set up, you can access the AWS Management Console.

b. Configuring AWS Cognito for User Authentication

1. **Create a Cognito User Pool**: In the AWS Management Console, navigate to the Cognito service and create a new user pool for managing user authentication.
2. **Configure App Client**: Create an app client within the user pool. Note the App Client ID, as you will need it for your front-end application.
3. **Set Up User Attributes**: Configure the user attributes (e.g., email, password) that users will provide during registration.
4. **Enable Authentication Flows**: Enable the appropriate authentication flows, such as username/password authentication.

c. Creating a DynamoDB Table for Tasks

1. **Create a DynamoDB Table**: In the AWS Management Console, navigate to DynamoDB and create a new table named "Tasks." Define the primary key as "taskId" (string) to uniquely identify tasks.
2. **Set Up Table Attributes**: Define additional attributes for your tasks, such as "userId," "taskName," and "completed."

d. Setting Up AWS Lambda Functions

1. **Create a Lambda Function**: In the AWS Management Console, navigate to Lambda and create a new function. Choose "Author from scratch" and give it a name like "TaskFunction."

2. **Configure the Function**: Set up the execution role that grants permissions to access DynamoDB and Cognito. Use the AWS managed policy "AmazonDynamoDBFullAccess" for simplicity.

3. **Write the Function Code**: Implement the necessary CRUD operations in the Lambda function. For this example, we will create a basic handler for task management.

4. Here's a simple example of a Lambda function handling task operations:

```javascript
Copy code
const AWS = require('aws-sdk');
const docClient = new AWS.
DynamoDB.DocumentClient();

exports.handler = async (event) => {
const httpMethod = event.httpMethod;
const path = event.path;
const response = {
statusCode: 200,
body: JSON.stringify
({ message: 'Success' }),
    };

    switch (httpMethod) {
case 'GET':
if (path === '/tasks') {
// Retrieve all tasks
const tasks = await getTasks();
response.body = JSON.stringify(tasks);
    }
 break;
case 'POST':
if (path === '/tasks') {
```

```
 const task = JSON.parse(event.body);
await createTask(task);
response.body = JSON.stringify(task);
              }
break;
// Implement additional cases
for PUT and DELETE as needed
    }

return response;
};


const getTasks = async () => {
const params = {
TableName: 'Tasks',
    };
const result = await
docClient.scan(params).promise();
return result.Items;
};


const createTask = async (task) => {
const params = {
TableName: 'Tasks',
Item: {
taskId: task.taskId,
userId: task.userId,
taskName: task.taskName,
completed: task.completed,
        },
    };
await docClient.put
(params).promise();
};
```

1. **Deploy the Function**: Deploy the Lambda function and note its ARN (Amazon Resource Name) for later use.

e. Setting Up API Gateway

1. **Create an API**: In the AWS Management Console, navigate to API Gateway and create a new REST API.
2. **Define Resources**: Create resources for tasks (e.g., /tasks) and define methods for handling HTTP requests (GET, POST, etc.).
3. **Integrate with Lambda**: For each method, integrate the API with the corresponding Lambda function. This allows API Gateway to trigger the Lambda function when requests are made.
4. **Deploy the API**: Deploy the API to a stage (e.g., "prod") and note the endpoint URL for accessing the API.

5. Implementing the Front-End with React

a. Setting Up the User Interface

1. **Create Components**: Within your React application, create components for task management, such as TaskList, TaskForm, and TaskItem.
2. **Integrate AWS Cognito**: Use the AWS SDK to implement user authentication with Cognito. Create a login and registration form that interacts with the Cognito user pool.
3. **Fetch and Display Tasks**: In the TaskList component, fetch tasks from the API using the endpoint provided by API Gateway. Display the tasks in a list format.

b. Example Code for the Task List Component
Here's an example of how to implement the TaskList component:

```javascript
Copy code
import React, { useState, useEffect }
from 'react';
import { API } from 'aws-amplify';
```

```
const TaskList = () => {
const [tasks, setTasks] = useState([]);

useEffect(() => {
const fetchTasks = async () => {
try {
const response = await API.
get('YourApiName', '/tasks');
setTasks(response);
} catch (error) {
console.error('Error
fetching tasks:', error);
            }
        };

fetchTasks();
    }, []);

return (
        <div>
<h2>Your Tasks</h2>
      <ul>
{tasks.map(task => (
<li key={task.taskId}>
{task.taskName}</li>
              ))}
          </ul>
      </div>
    );
};

export default TaskList;
```

6. Testing the Full-Stack Application

a. Local Testing

Before deploying the application, it's essential to test it locally. Use tools like Jest or React Testing Library to write unit tests for your React components.

- **Test User Authentication**: Ensure that user authentication works as expected, including registration, login, and session management.
- **Test API Calls**: Mock API calls in your tests to verify that the front end correctly interacts with the back end.

b. End-to-End Testing

Conduct end-to-end testing to validate the entire application workflow. Tools like Cypress or Selenium can be used for this purpose.

- **Test User Flows**: Simulate user interactions to ensure that the application behaves as expected throughout the task management process.
- **Monitor Performance**: Assess the performance of the application during testing to identify any bottlenecks or latency issues.

7. Deploying the Full-Stack Application

a. Deploying the Front-End

Once testing is complete, deploy the front-end application. Depending on your chosen stack, you can use services like AWS Amplify, Netlify, or Vercel to host the React application.

- **AWS Amplify Hosting**: If using AWS Amplify, follow the deployment process to host the front-end application. Amplify automatically handles the build and deployment pipeline.

b. Deploying the Back-End

Ensure that the back-end components are properly configured in the AWS environment. Deploy the API Gateway, Lambda functions, and DynamoDB table as necessary.

- **API Gateway Configuration**: Ensure that the API Gateway is correctly configured to handle requests and route them to the appropriate Lambda functions.

8. Monitoring and Maintaining the Application

a. Monitoring Performance

After deployment, it's essential to monitor the performance of the full-stack application continuously. Utilize tools like AWS CloudWatch to track key metrics such as response times, error rates, and usage patterns.

- **Set Up Alerts**: Configure alerts to notify the development team of any performance issues or anomalies in real-time.

b. Maintenance and Updates

Regularly maintain and update the application to ensure optimal performance and security. Implement a CI/CD pipeline to automate the deployment of updates.

- **Automated Testing**: Integrate automated testing into the CI/CD pipeline to ensure that changes do not introduce new issues.
- **Version Control**: Use version control to manage code changes and facilitate collaboration among team members.

9. Lessons Learned from Building a Serverless Full-Stack Application

Building a full-stack application using serverless architecture offers valuable insights and lessons:

1. **Focus on User Experience**: Prioritize user experience in both the front-

end and back-end design. Ensure that the application is responsive, intuitive, and performant.

2. **Leverage Managed Services**: Utilize managed cloud services to reduce operational overhead and streamline development processes. This allows teams to focus on building features rather than managing infrastructure.

3. **Implement Security Best Practices**: Security should be a top priority throughout the development lifecycle. Implement best practices for authentication, data protection, and secure API design.

4. **Test Early and Often**: Establish a robust testing strategy that includes unit testing, integration testing, and end-to-end testing. Testing early in the development process helps identify issues before they reach production.

5. **Embrace Continuous Improvement**: Continuously monitor application performance and user feedback. Be open to making improvements and iterating on features based on user needs and market trends.

Conclusion

Building a complete full-stack application using serverless architecture offers numerous benefits, including scalability, cost efficiency, and reduced operational overhead. By leveraging managed cloud services and following best practices for development, testing, and deployment, organizations can create high-quality applications that meet user needs.

This chapter provided a comprehensive guide to building a full-stack serverless application, covering everything from defining requirements to deploying the final product. As serverless technology continues to evolve, organizations that embrace this architecture will be well-positioned to innovate and deliver exceptional user experiences in the rapidly changing digital landscape.

As we move forward, organizations can harness the power of serverless computing to streamline development processes, enhance agility, and drive meaningful outcomes. The insights gained from this chapter can serve as a roadmap for building robust, efficient, and scalable applications in an increasingly competitive market.

Chapter 15: Key Takeaways and Future Directions in Serverless Computing

As we conclude this comprehensive exploration of serverless computing, it is essential to reflect on the key takeaways and consider the future directions of this evolving technology. Serverless architecture has become a significant paradigm shift in how applications are developed, deployed, and managed. This chapter aims to summarize the critical insights gained throughout this book and discuss the potential future developments and trends that may shape the serverless landscape in the years to come.

Key Takeaways from the Serverless Journey

1. Understanding Serverless Architecture

Serverless computing represents a shift from traditional infrastructure management to a model where cloud providers handle the underlying infrastructure. This abstraction allows developers to focus on writing code and delivering features without worrying about server management. Key characteristics of serverless architecture include:

- **Event-Driven Execution**: Serverless functions are triggered by events, allowing for dynamic scaling and responsive applications.

- **Stateless Functions**: Each function invocation is stateless, meaning it does not retain any context from previous invocations. This allows for easy scaling and high availability.
- **Managed Services**: Serverless architecture leverages various managed services (e.g., databases, storage, authentication) to streamline development and reduce operational overhead.

2. Benefits of Serverless Computing

The advantages of adopting serverless architecture are numerous and compelling:

- **Cost Efficiency**: Organizations pay only for the actual compute time consumed, leading to significant cost savings compared to traditional hosting models.
- **Scalability**: Serverless architectures automatically scale to accommodate varying workloads, allowing applications to handle spikes in traffic without manual intervention.
- **Faster Time to Market**: By abstracting away infrastructure management, teams can deploy new features more rapidly, enhancing agility and competitiveness.

3. Best Practices for Serverless Development

Implementing best practices is crucial for successfully building and deploying serverless applications. Key best practices include:

- **Embrace Microservices**: Adopting a microservices architecture allows for flexibility, scalability, and independent deployment of application components.
- **Focus on Security**: Security should be prioritized at every stage of development. Implementing secure coding practices, authentication, and

access controls is essential for protecting sensitive data.

- **Implement Robust Monitoring**: Continuous monitoring of application performance and health is crucial for identifying issues and ensuring reliability.

4. Testing and Debugging in Serverless Environments

Testing and debugging are critical aspects of serverless application development. Organizations should:

- **Adopt Automated Testing**: Automated testing helps ensure that applications function as intended and can be rapidly iterated upon without introducing new issues.
- **Utilize Logging and Tracing**: Effective logging and tracing mechanisms provide insights into application behavior, enabling teams to diagnose and troubleshoot issues efficiently.
- **Focus on End-to-End Testing**: Comprehensive end-to-end testing validates the entire application workflow, ensuring a seamless user experience.

5. Real-World Case Studies

Throughout this book, various case studies demonstrated the practical applications of serverless computing across industries. Key lessons learned from these case studies include:

- **Adaptability**: Organizations that embraced serverless architectures demonstrated increased agility and adaptability to changing market demands.
- **Innovation**: Leveraging serverless technology enabled companies to innovate rapidly and deliver new features to customers faster.
- **User-Centric Design**: Focusing on user experience and performance led to higher levels of customer satisfaction and engagement.

Future Directions in Serverless Computing

As serverless computing continues to evolve, several trends and innovations are expected to shape its future. Understanding these potential developments will help organizations prepare for the next phase of their serverless journey.

1. Integration with Edge Computing

The convergence of serverless computing and edge computing is likely to play a significant role in the future. Edge computing allows for processing data closer to the source, reducing latency and improving response times.

- **Improved User Experience**: By deploying serverless functions at the edge, organizations can deliver content and services with minimal latency, enhancing the overall user experience.
- **Real-Time Processing**: Serverless architectures combined with edge computing can facilitate real-time data processing, enabling organizations to make immediate decisions based on incoming data.

2. Enhanced Security Features

As serverless computing becomes more widely adopted, the focus on security will intensify. Cloud providers are expected to invest in enhanced security features to protect serverless applications from evolving threats.

- **Automated Security Scanning**: Tools for automatically scanning serverless applications for vulnerabilities will become more sophisticated, helping organizations identify and mitigate risks proactively.
- **Built-in Security Controls**: Cloud platforms will likely continue to integrate security controls into the deployment process, making it easier for developers to implement best practices.

3. Advancements in Developer Tools

The development experience is critical to the adoption of serverless computing. As the technology matures, we can expect advancements in developer tools that streamline the development, testing, and deployment processes.

- **Local Development Environments**: Tools that facilitate local development and testing of serverless functions will become increasingly important, allowing developers to build and debug applications efficiently.
- **Improved Frameworks**: Serverless frameworks will continue to evolve, providing enhanced abstractions and features that simplify the development workflow.

4. Multi-Cloud and Hybrid Architectures

As organizations seek to avoid vendor lock-in and enhance resilience, multi-cloud and hybrid architectures will become more prevalent in serverless computing.

- **Interoperability Solutions**: The demand for tools and frameworks that enable seamless integration across multiple cloud providers will grow. Organizations will benefit from being able to leverage the best features of different platforms.
- **Data Management**: Managing data across multiple cloud environments will present challenges. Innovations in data synchronization and integration will be crucial for successful multi-cloud strategies.

5. Growth of Event-Driven Architectures

The adoption of event-driven architectures is expected to increase as organizations recognize the benefits of building applications that respond to events in real-time.

- **Event Streaming Technologies**: Tools and technologies for event streaming (e.g., Apache Kafka, Amazon Kinesis) will play a significant role in facilitating event-driven architectures, enabling real-time data processing and analytics.
- **Microservices Integration**: Event-driven architectures will enhance the integration between microservices, allowing for more flexible and scalable applications.

6. Expanding Use Cases for Serverless Computing

As serverless technology matures, new use cases will emerge across various industries. Some potential use cases include:

- **Machine Learning and AI**: Serverless architectures will increasingly be used for data preprocessing, model training, and inference, enabling organizations to leverage AI capabilities without managing infrastructure.
- **IoT Applications**: The demand for serverless computing in IoT applications will grow, allowing organizations to process and analyze data generated by connected devices in real-time.

Conclusion

The journey through serverless computing has revealed its transformative potential for application development and deployment. Organizations that embrace serverless architecture can enjoy numerous benefits, including scalability, cost efficiency, and reduced operational overhead.

As we look to the future, it is clear that serverless computing will continue to evolve, driven by advancements in technology, changing market demands, and emerging use cases. By understanding the key takeaways and anticipating future directions, organizations can position themselves for success in the ever-changing landscape of software development.

In conclusion, serverless computing is not just a trend; it is a powerful paradigm that will shape the future of application development. As organizations continue to innovate and adapt, the insights gained from this exploration will serve as a valuable resource for navigating the complexities of serverless architectures and driving meaningful outcomes in an increasingly digital world. Embracing the principles of serverless computing will empower organizations to build robust, efficient, and scalable applications that meet the evolving needs of users and the market.

Conclusion: Embracing the Future of Serverless Computing

S
erverless computing represents a paradigm shift in how applications are developed, deployed, and managed. As organizations increasingly recognize the benefits of serverless architectures—such as scalability, cost efficiency, and reduced operational overhead—their adoption has accelerated across various industries. The exploration of serverless computing throughout this book has highlighted its transformative potential and provided valuable insights into its practical applications, benefits, challenges, and future directions.

The Transformative Potential of Serverless Computing

Serverless computing allows organizations to focus on what matters most: delivering value to users through innovative applications. By abstracting away infrastructure management, developers can concentrate on writing code, building features, and enhancing user experiences. The benefits of serverless architecture are numerous:

1. **Scalability**: One of the most significant advantages of serverless computing is its ability to scale automatically in response to varying workloads. This dynamic scaling capability ensures that applications

can handle spikes in traffic without requiring manual intervention or complex provisioning processes.

2. **Cost Efficiency**: With a pay-as-you-go pricing model, serverless computing allows organizations to pay only for the resources they use. This cost-effective approach is particularly beneficial for applications with unpredictable traffic patterns, as it eliminates the need for over-provisioning.

3. **Faster Time to Market**: The rapid development and deployment cycles facilitated by serverless architectures empower organizations to bring new features and applications to market faster. This agility is critical in today's competitive landscape, where organizations must respond quickly to changing customer demands and market conditions.

Key Insights and Best Practices

Throughout this book, we explored numerous case studies and best practices that can guide organizations in their serverless journey. Some of the key insights include:

- **Embracing Microservices**: The adoption of a microservices architecture enhances flexibility and scalability. By breaking applications into smaller, manageable components, organizations can deploy and update services independently, reducing the risk of widespread failures.
- **Prioritizing Security**: As serverless computing gains popularity, security must remain a top priority. Organizations should implement best practices for authentication, authorization, and data protection to safeguard their applications.
- **Investing in Monitoring and Observability**: Continuous monitoring and observability are essential for maintaining application health and performance. Organizations should leverage tools and practices that provide real-time insights into application behavior, enabling them to identify and address issues proactively.
- **Testing and Debugging**: Effective testing and debugging practices are

crucial for ensuring the reliability of serverless applications. Organizations should adopt automated testing strategies and implement robust logging and tracing mechanisms to facilitate troubleshooting.

Future Directions in Serverless Computing

The future of serverless computing is bright, with several trends and innovations expected to shape its evolution:

1. **Integration with Edge Computing**: The convergence of serverless and edge computing will enhance performance and reduce latency for applications that require real-time processing. Deploying serverless functions at the edge will enable organizations to deliver content and services closer to users, improving overall user experience.

2. **Advancements in Developer Tools**: As serverless technology matures, the development experience will continue to improve. Enhanced frameworks, local development environments, and automated deployment tools will streamline the development process and make it easier for teams to build and manage serverless applications.

3. **Expanding Use Cases**: New use cases for serverless computing are emerging across various industries. From IoT applications to machine learning workflows, organizations are discovering innovative ways to leverage serverless technology to meet their unique needs.

4. **Focus on Multi-Cloud Strategies**: As organizations seek to avoid vendor lock-in, multi-cloud strategies will become more prevalent. Tools and frameworks that enable seamless integration across different cloud providers will be essential for organizations looking to optimize their serverless architectures.

The Path Forward

As organizations navigate the complexities of building and deploying serverless applications, the insights gained from this exploration will serve as a valuable resource. Embracing the principles of serverless computing will empower organizations to build robust, efficient, and scalable applications that meet the evolving needs of users and the market.

In conclusion, serverless computing is not just a fleeting trend; it is a powerful and transformative paradigm that will shape the future of application development. By adopting serverless architectures, organizations can enhance their agility, innovate rapidly, and drive meaningful outcomes in an increasingly digital world. As the technology continues to evolve, those who embrace serverless computing will be well-positioned to thrive in the competitive landscape, delivering exceptional user experiences and achieving sustainable growth.

www.ingramcontent.com/pod-product-compliance
Lightning Source LLC
Chambersburg PA
CBHW071458220526
45472CB00003B/841